For Daniel Lavoie,
in memory of Guillaume

PHILIPPE GIRARD

# OBITUARY MAN

TRANSLATION BY KERRYANN COCHRANE

BDANG

Originally published in French as LA VISITE DES MORTS: © 2010 Les Éditions Glénat Québec Inc

TRANSLATION BY KERRYANN COCHRANE

Printed by Gauvin Press in Gatineau, Quebec, Canada
BDANG Imprint edited by Andy Brown
BDANG logo by Billy Mavreas

First English Edition

Other titles by Philippe Girard in the BDANG series:
Ruts & Gullies: Nine Days in St Petersburg (ISBN 978-1-894994-46-0)
Killing Velazquez (ISBN 978-1-894994-54-5)

Library and Archives Canada Cataloguing in Publication
Girard, Philippe, 1971-
    Obituary man / Philippe Girard ; translated by KerryAnn Cochrane.

Translation of: La visite des morts.
ISBN 978-1-894994-70-5
    1. Graphic novels. I. Cochrane, KerryAnn II. Title.
PN6734.V57G5713 2013          j741.5'971          C2013-900366-5

Obituary Man is BDANG#11

CONUNDRUM PRESS
Greenwich, Nova Scotia, Canada
www.conundrumpress.com

Conundrum press acknowledges the financial support of the Canada Council for the Arts toward its publishing activities. We acknowledge the financial support of the Government of Canada, through the National Translation Program for Book Publishing, for our translation activities.

Canada Council    Conseil des Arts
for the Arts      du Canada

# Chapter 1

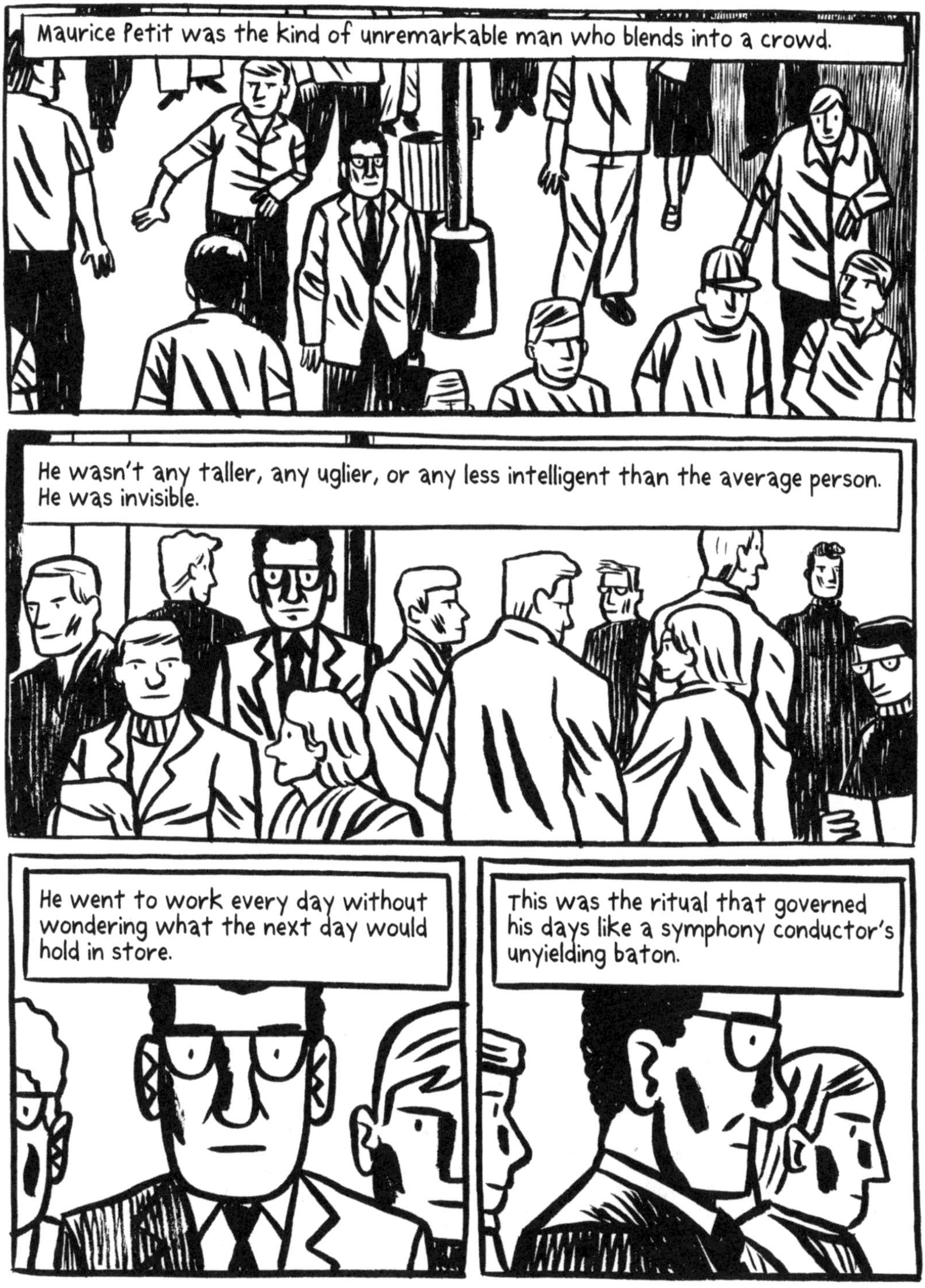
Maurice Petit was the kind of unremarkable man who blends into a crowd.
He wasn't any taller, any uglier, or any less intelligent than the average person. He was invisible.
He went to work every day without wondering what the next day would hold in store.
This was the ritual that governed his days like a symphony conductor's unyielding baton.

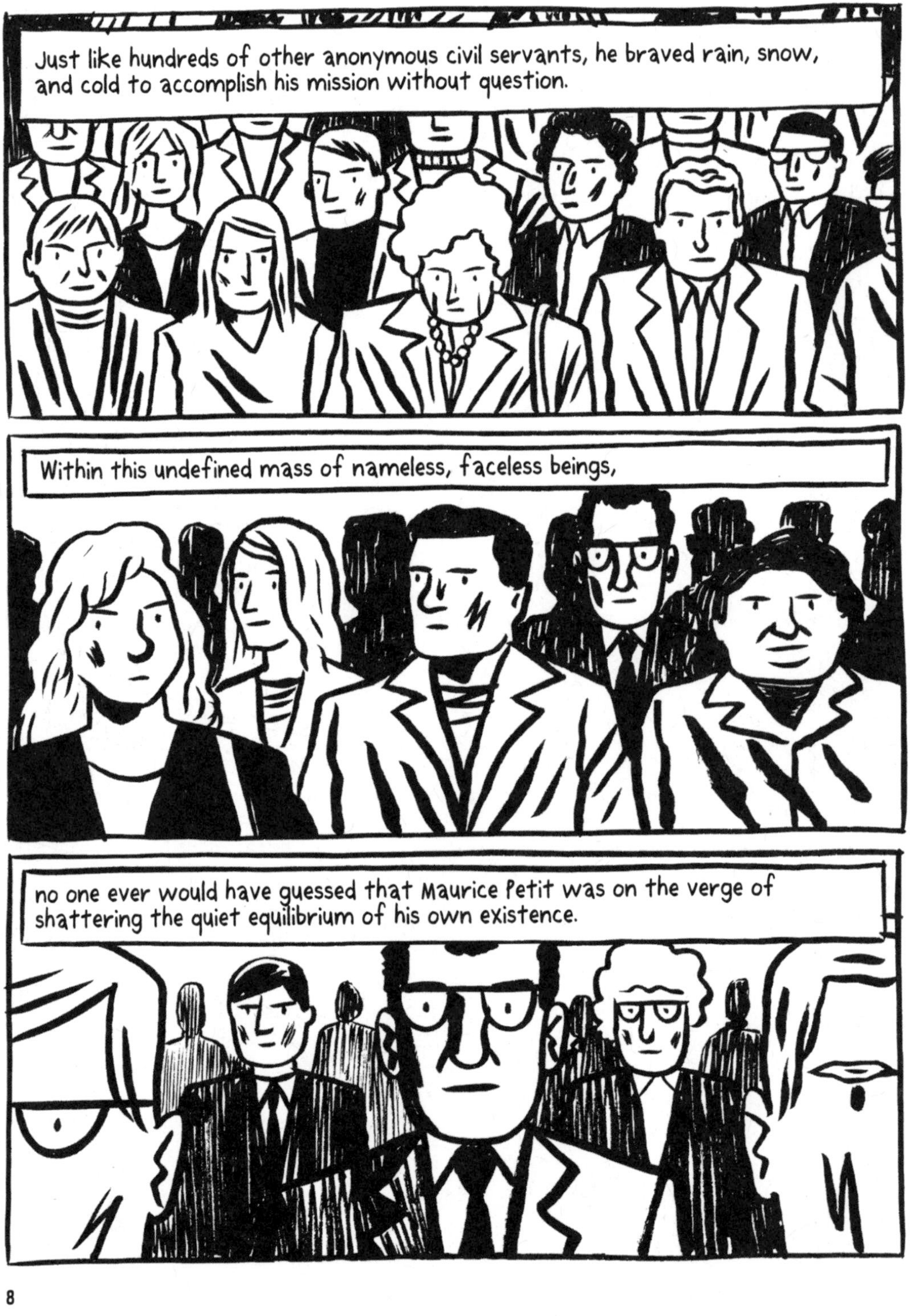
Just like hundreds of other anonymous civil servants, he braved rain, snow, and cold to accomplish his mission without question.
Within this undefined mass of nameless, faceless beings,
no one ever would have guessed that Maurice Petit was on the verge of shattering the quiet equilibrium of his own existence.

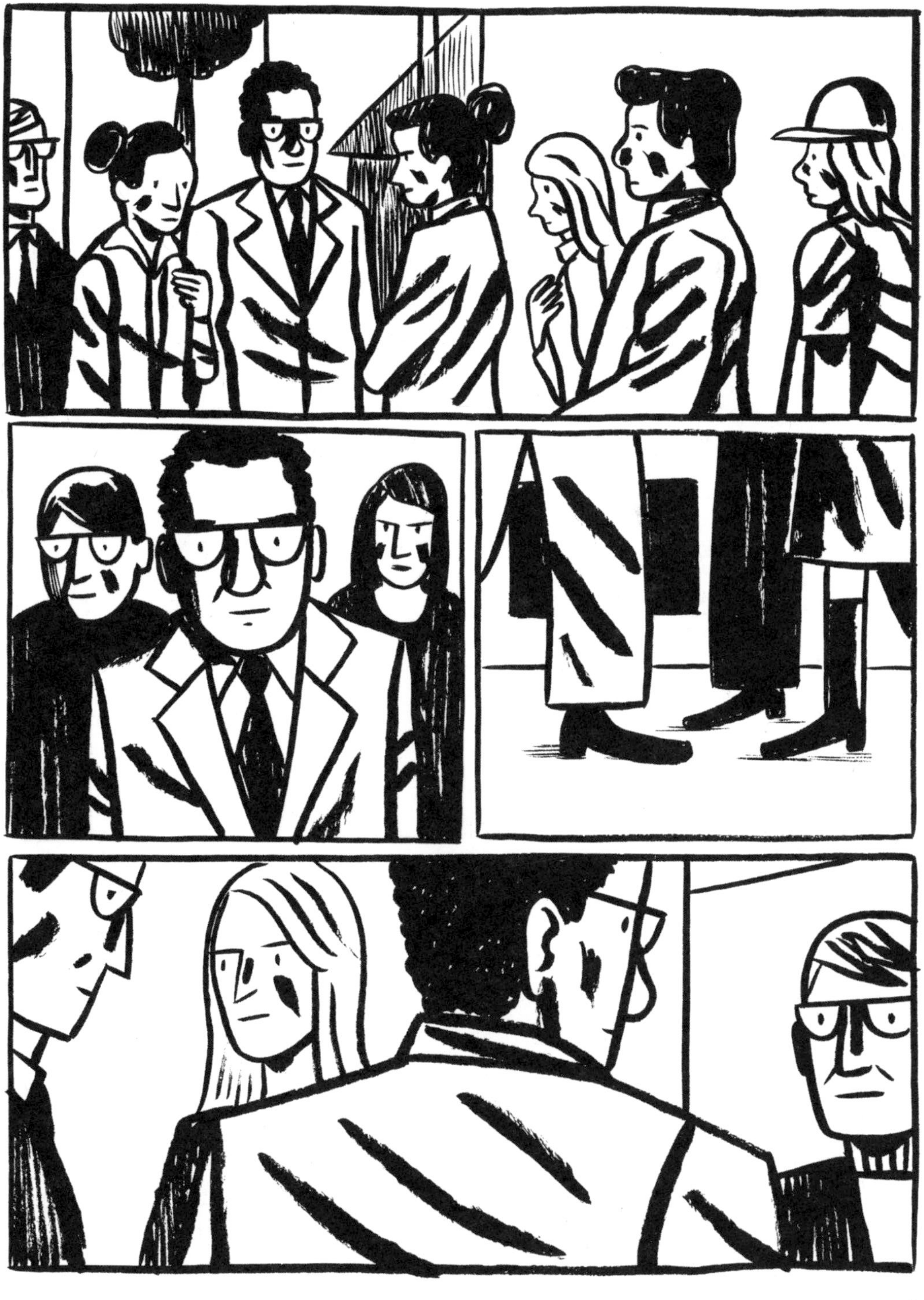

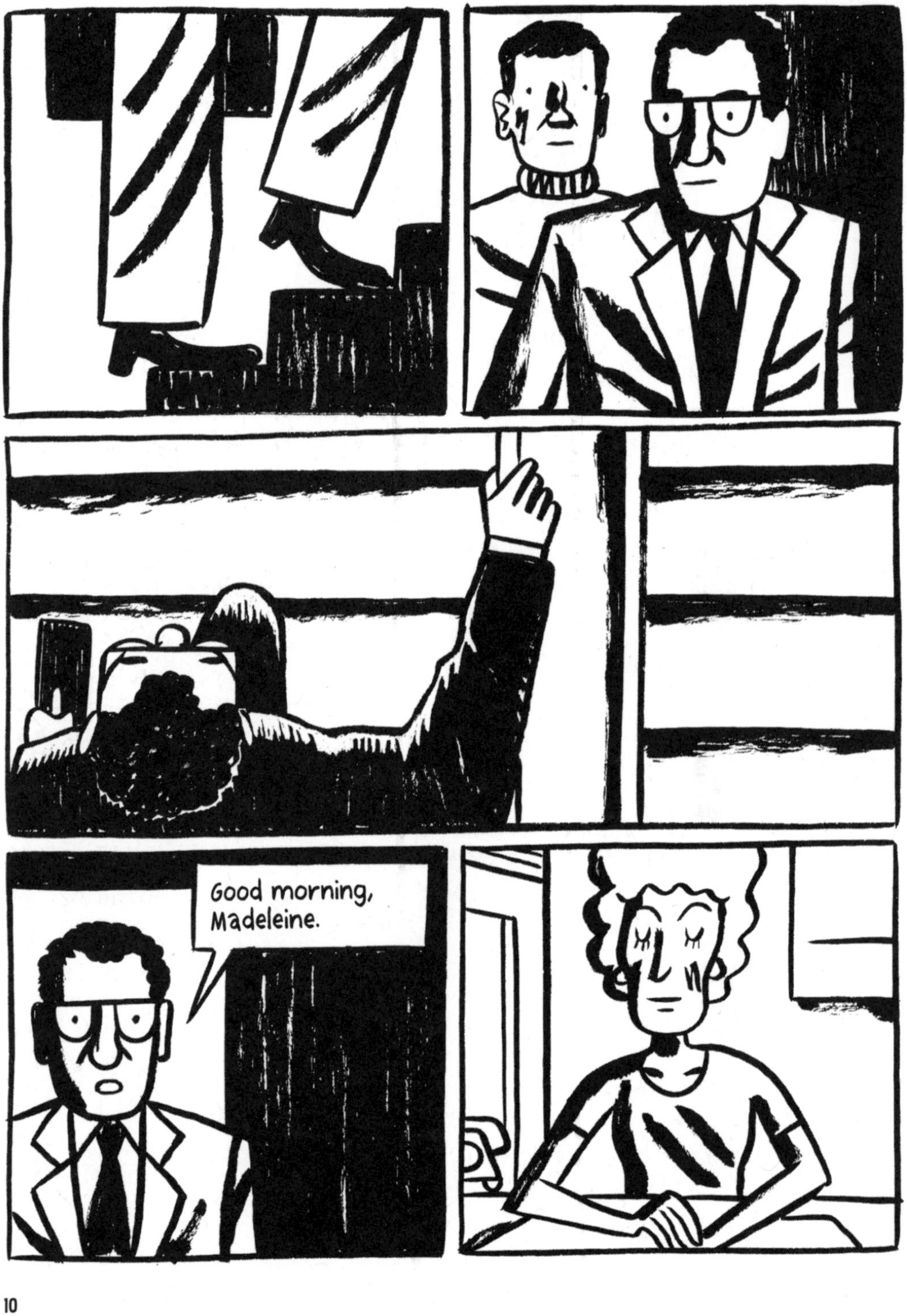
Good morning, Madeleine.

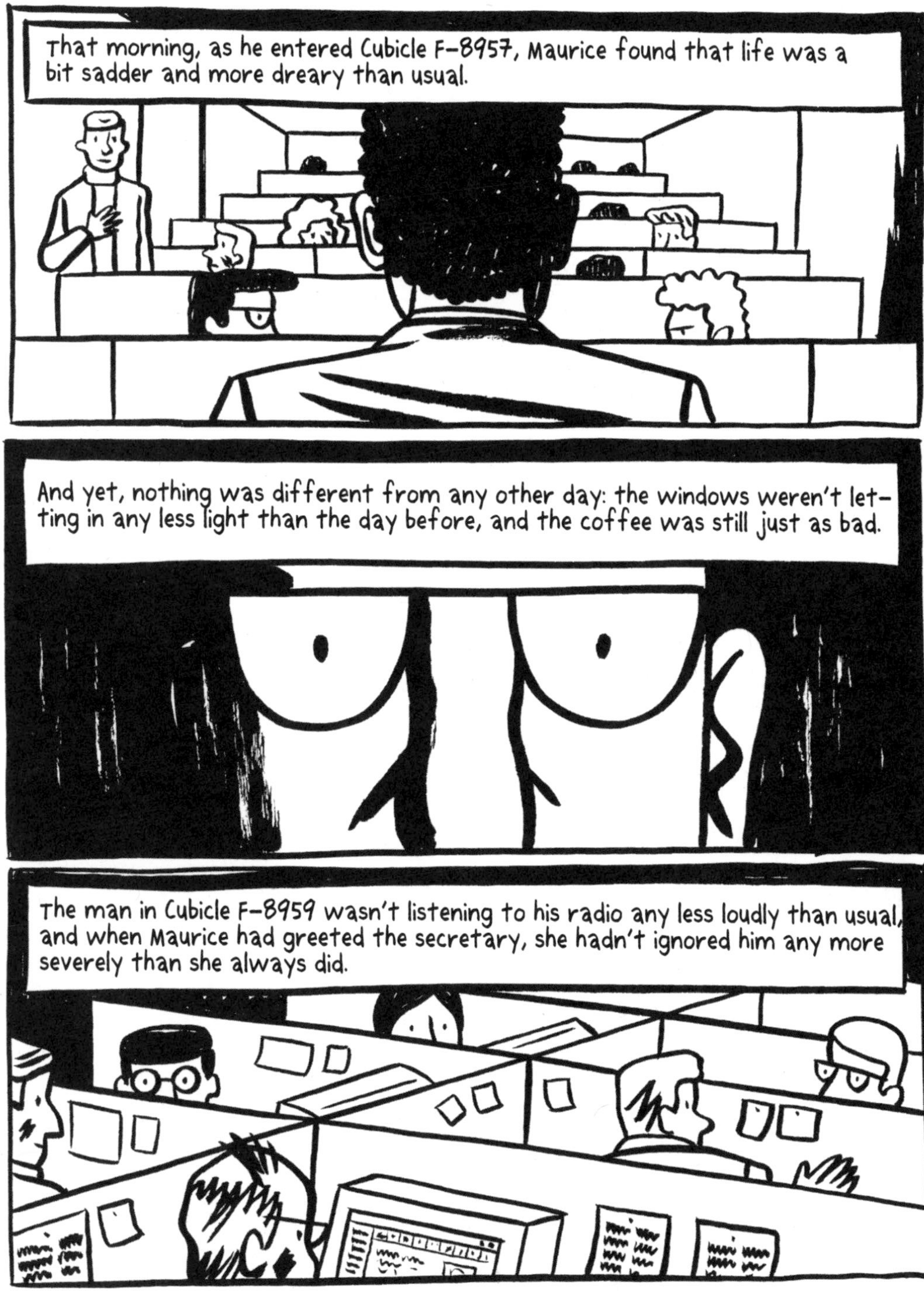
That morning, as he entered Cubicle F-8957, Maurice found that life was a bit sadder and more dreary than usual.
And yet, nothing was different from any other day: the windows weren't letting in any less light than the day before, and the coffee was still just as bad.
The man in Cubicle F-8959 wasn't listening to his radio any less loudly than usual, and when Maurice had greeted the secretary, she hadn't ignored him any more severely than she always did.

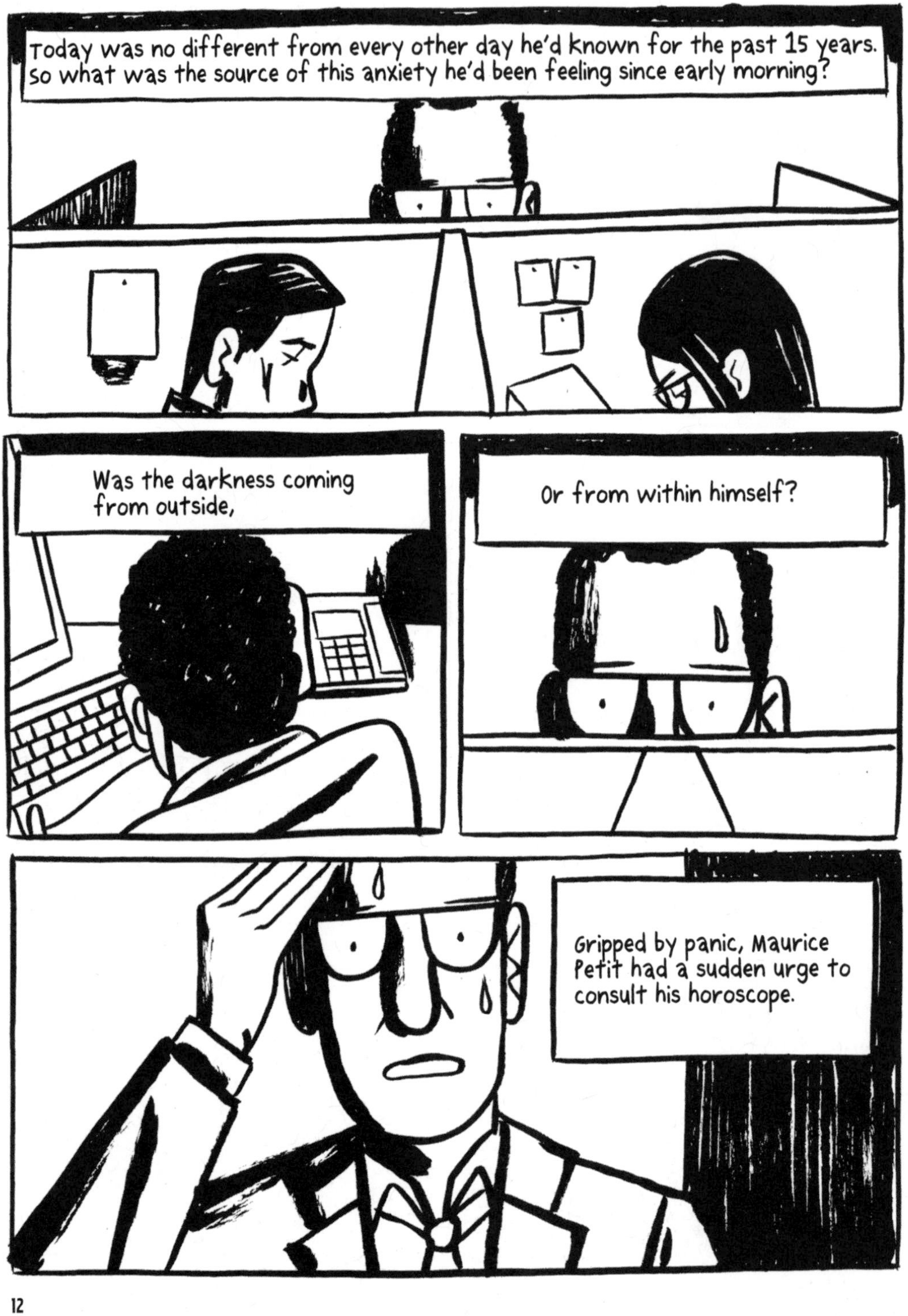
Today was no different from every other day he'd known for the past 15 years. So what was the source of this anxiety he'd been feeling since early morning?
Was the darkness coming from outside,
Or from within himself?
Gripped by panic, Maurice Petit had a sudden urge to consult his horoscope.

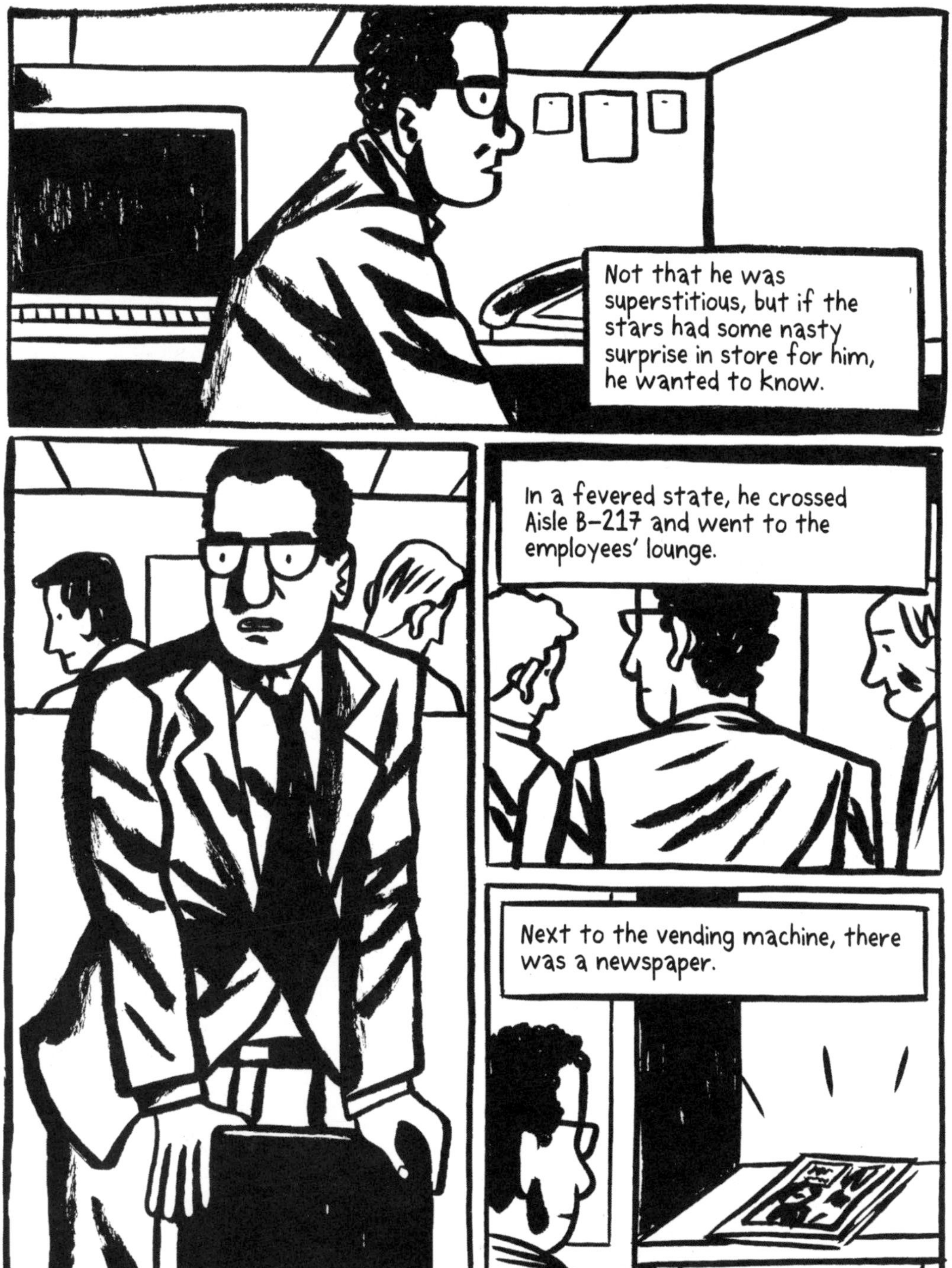
Not that he was superstitious, but if the stars had some nasty surprise in store for him, he wanted to know.
In a fevered state, he crossed Aisle B-217 and went to the employees' lounge.
Next to the vending machine, there was a newspaper.

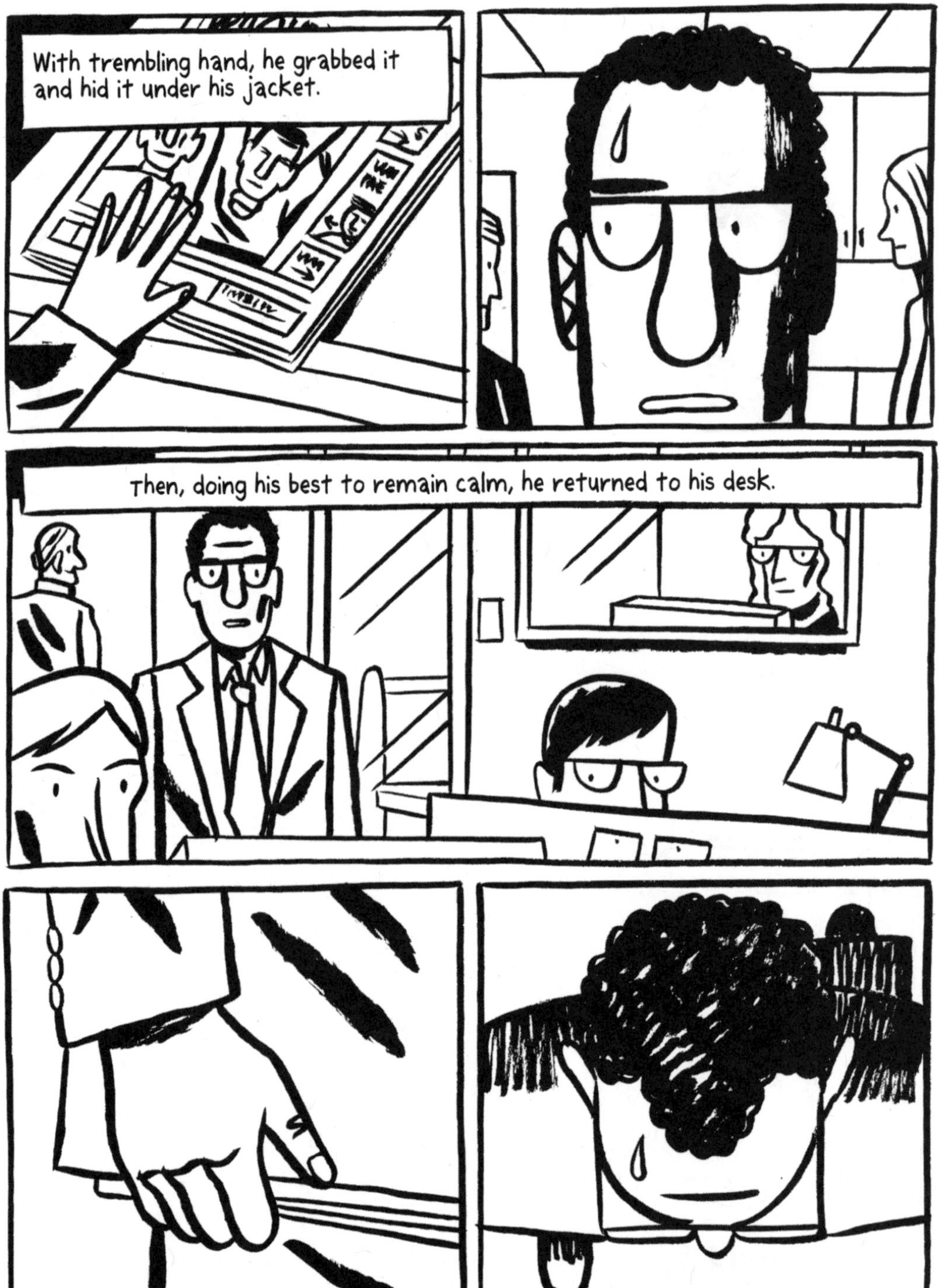
With trembling hand, he grabbed it and hid it under his jacket.
Then, doing his best to remain calm, he returned to his desk.

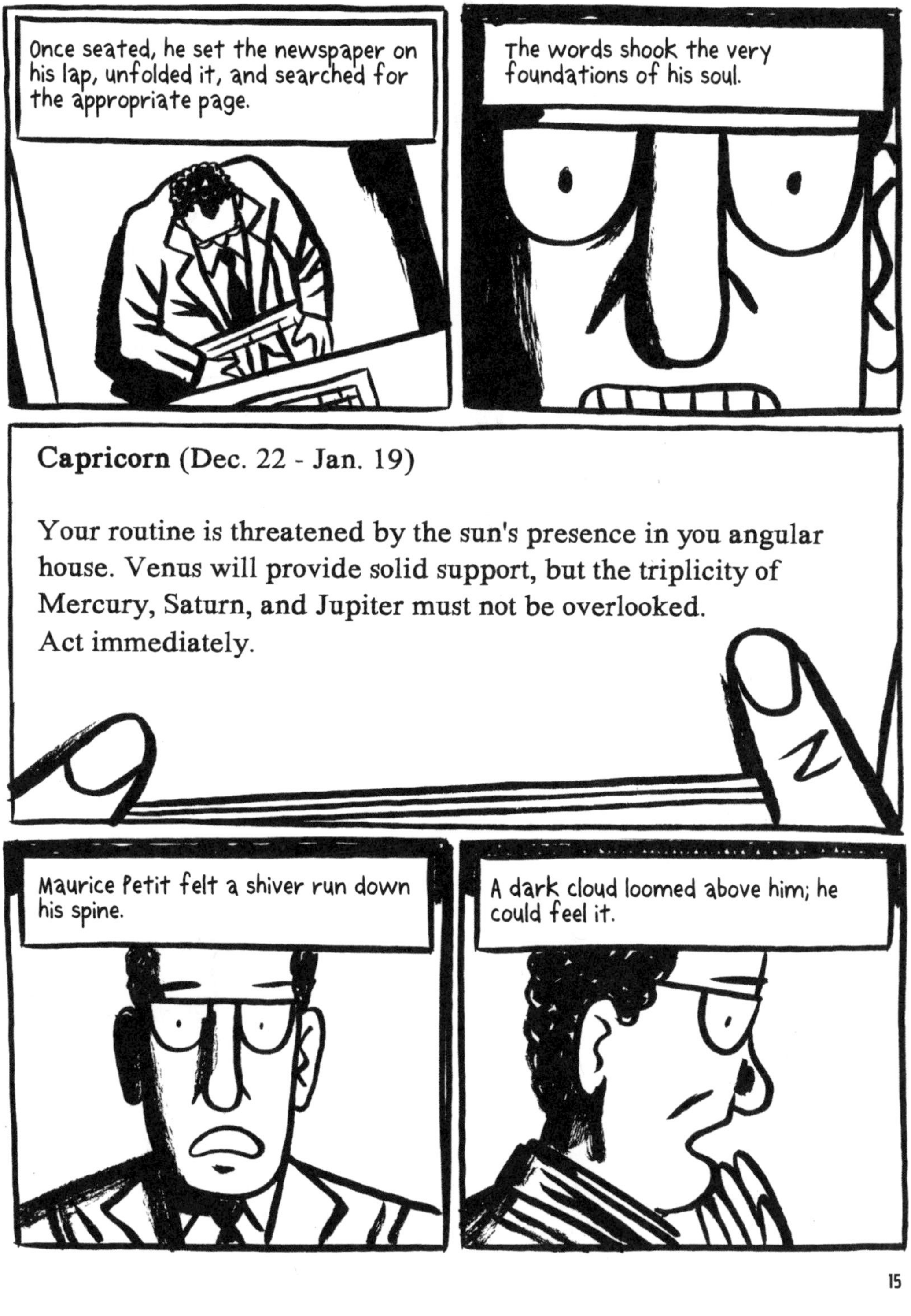
Once seated, he set the newspaper on his lap, unfolded it, and searched for the appropriate page.
The words shook the very foundations of his soul.
Capricorn (Dec. 22 - Jan. 19)
Your routine is threatened by the sun's presence in you angular house. Venus will provide solid support, but the triplicity of Mercury, Saturn, and Jupiter must not be overlooked. Act immediately.
Maurice Petit felt a shiver run down his spine.
A dark cloud loomed above him; he could feel it.

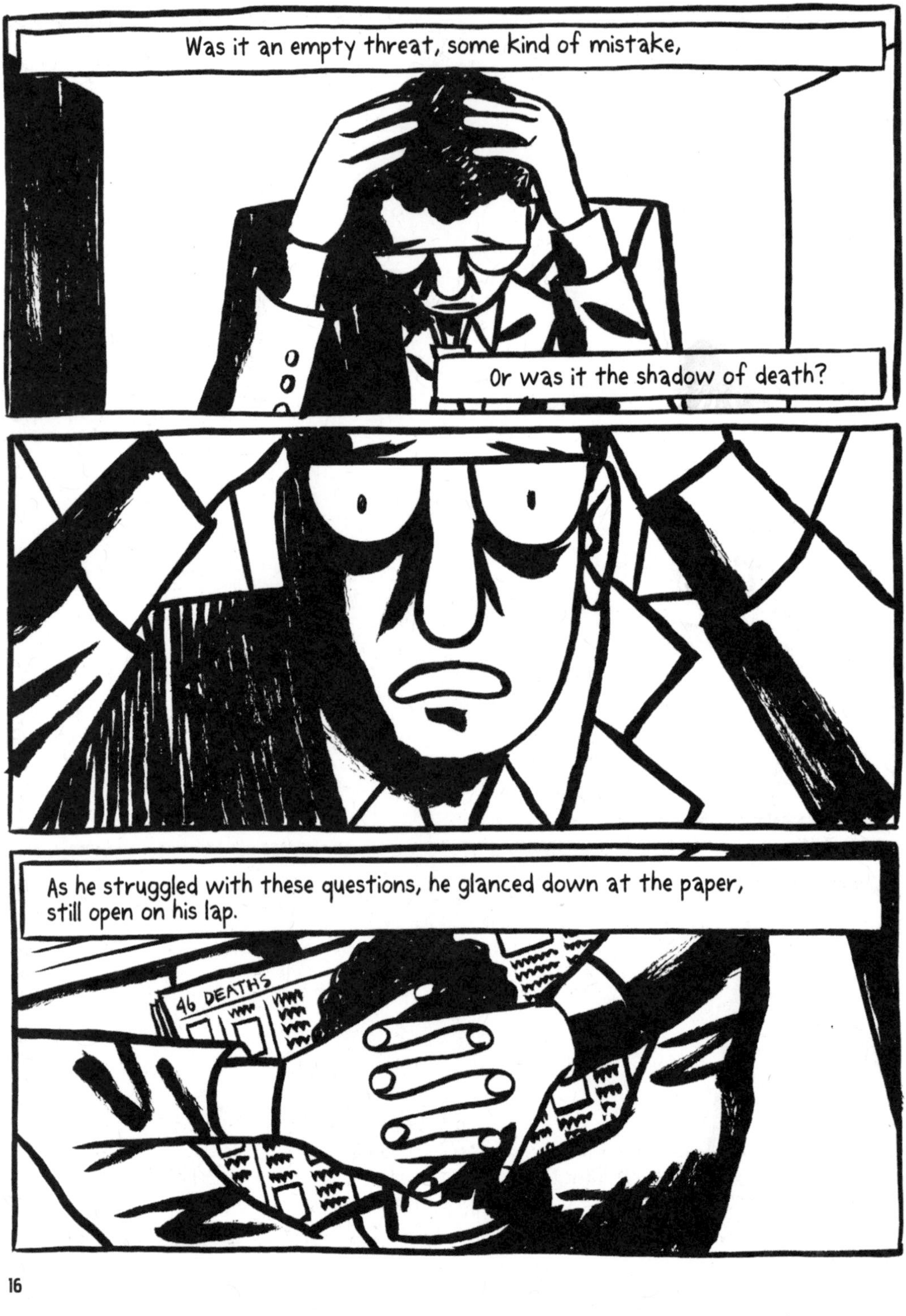
Was it an empty threat, some kind of mistake,
Or was it the shadow of death?
As he struggled with these questions, he glanced down at the paper, still open on his lap.
46 DEATHS

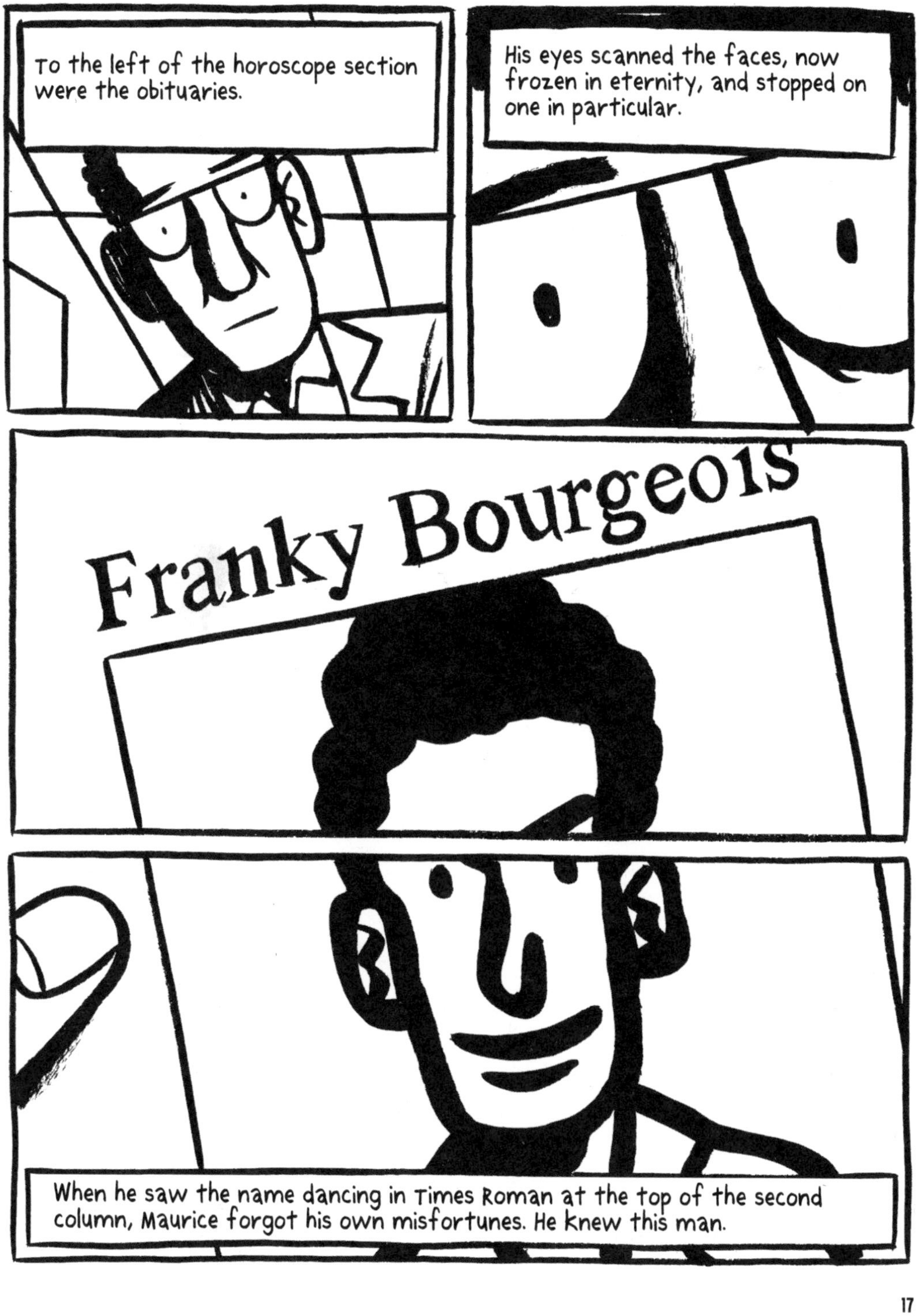
To the left of the horoscope section were the obituaries.
His eyes scanned the faces, now frozen in eternity, and stopped on one in particular.
Franky Bourgeois
When he saw the name dancing in Times Roman at the top of the second column, Maurice forgot his own misfortunes. He knew this man.

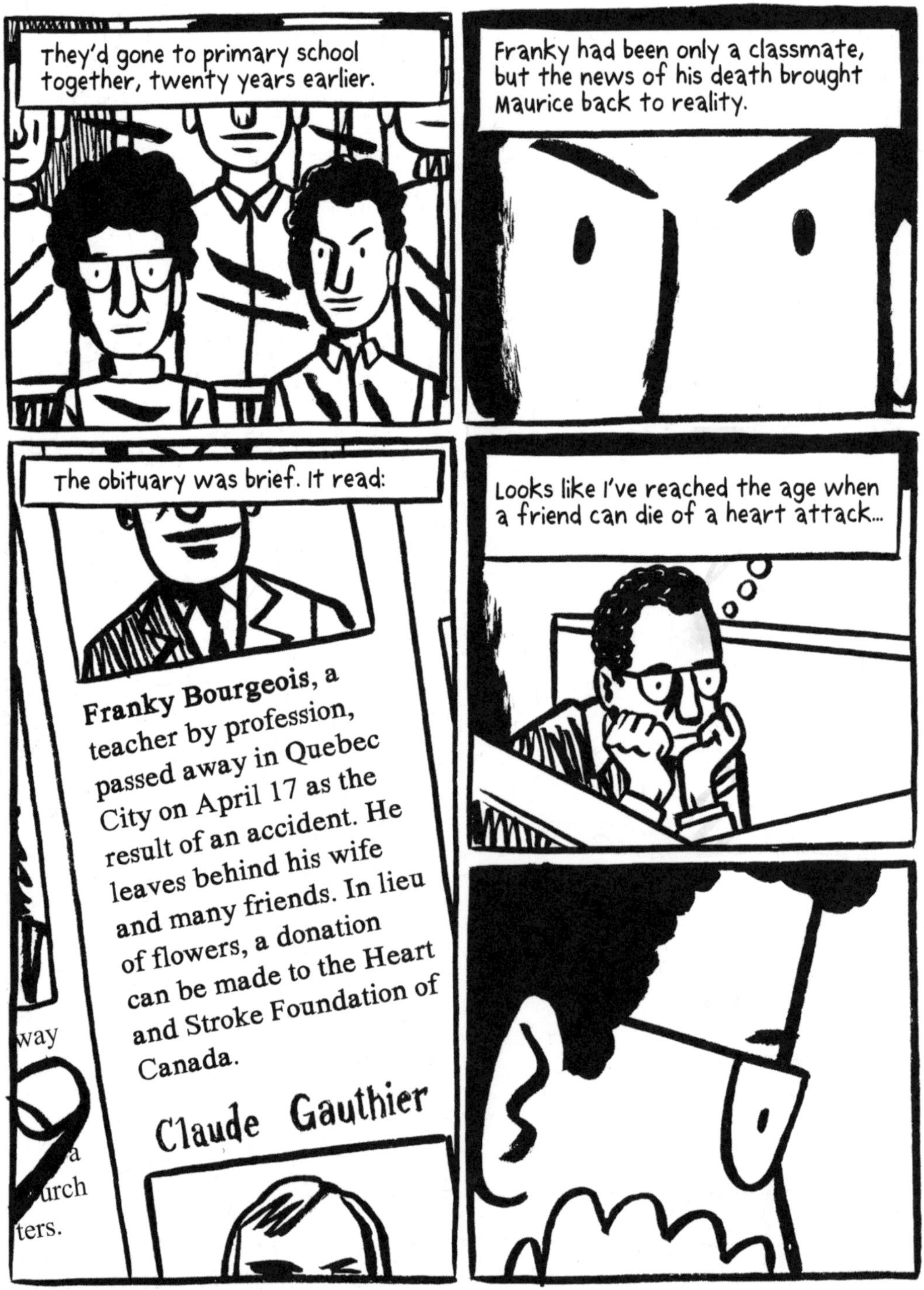
They'd gone to primary school together, twenty years earlier.
Franky had been only a classmate, but the news of his death brought Maurice back to reality.
The obituary was brief. It read:
Franky Bourgeois, a teacher by profession, passed away in Quebec City on April 17 as the result of an accident. He leaves behind his wife and many friends. In lieu of flowers, a donation can be made to the Heart and Stroke Foundation of Canada.
Claude Gauthier
Looks like I've reached the age when a friend can die of a heart attack...

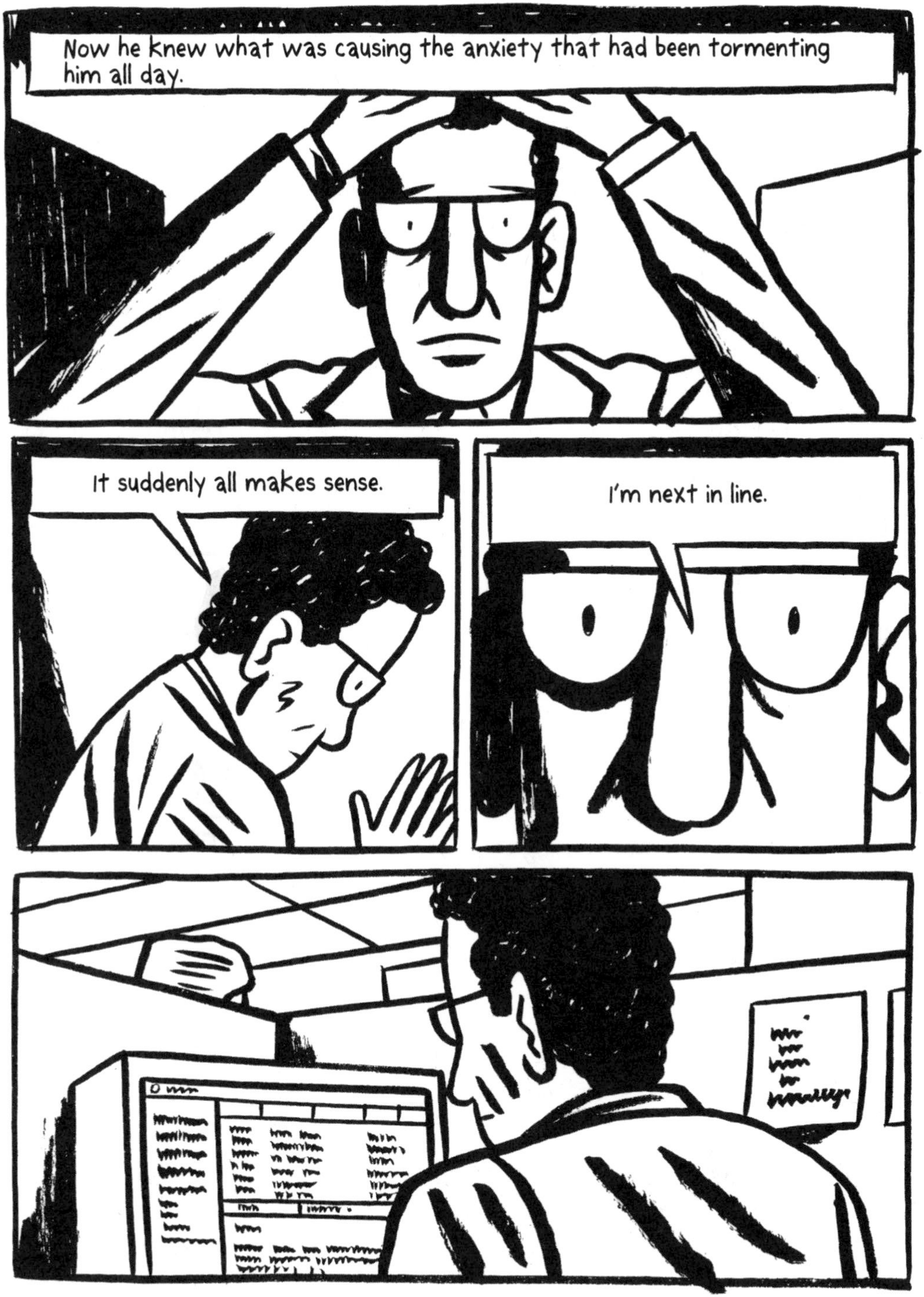
Now he knew what was causing the anxiety that had been tormenting him all day.
It suddenly all makes sense.
I'm next in line.

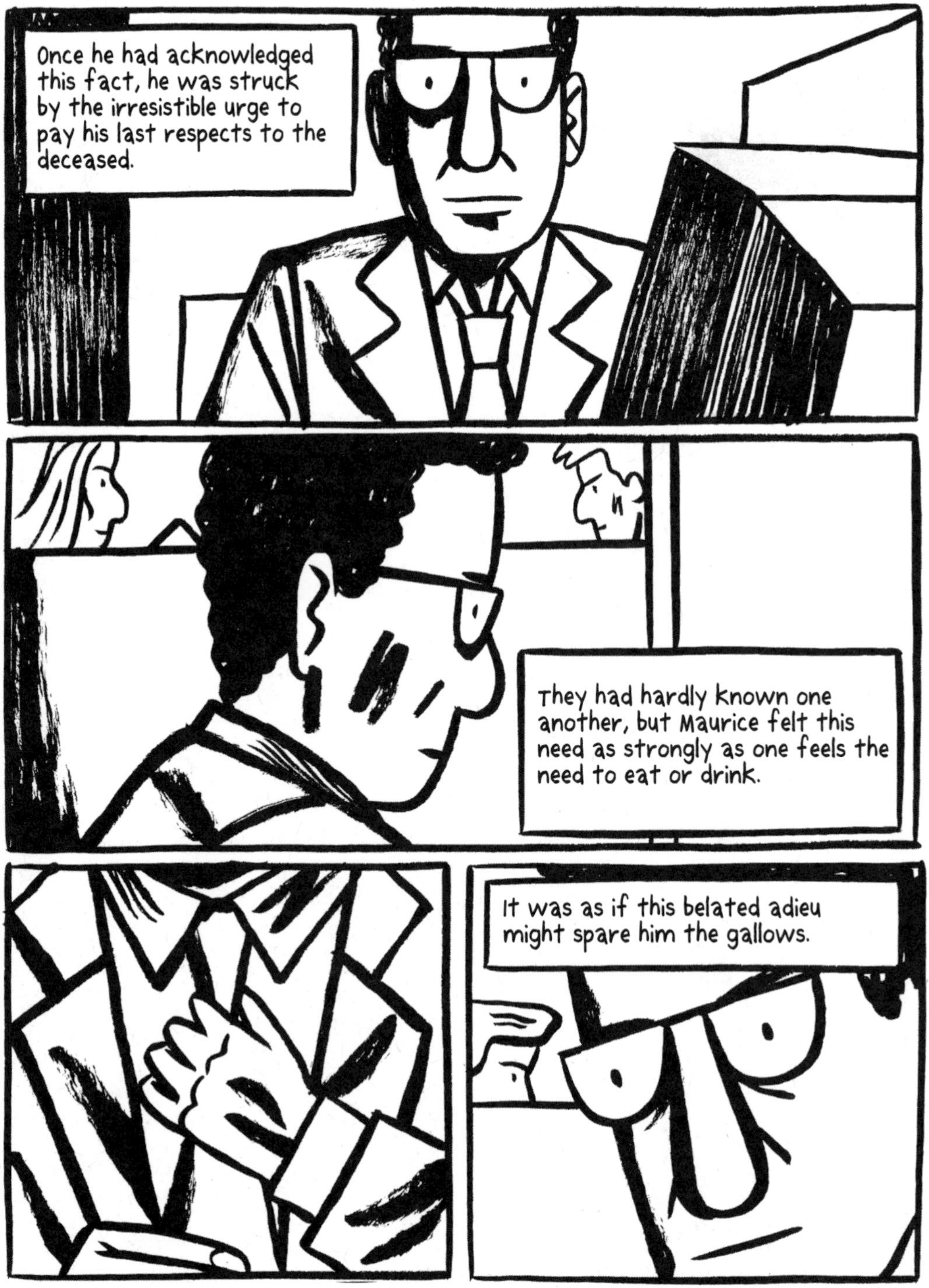
Once he had acknowledged this fact, he was struck by the irresistible urge to pay his last respects to the deceased.
They had hardly known one another, but Maurice felt this need as strongly as one feels the need to eat or drink.
It was as if this belated adieu might spare him the gallows.

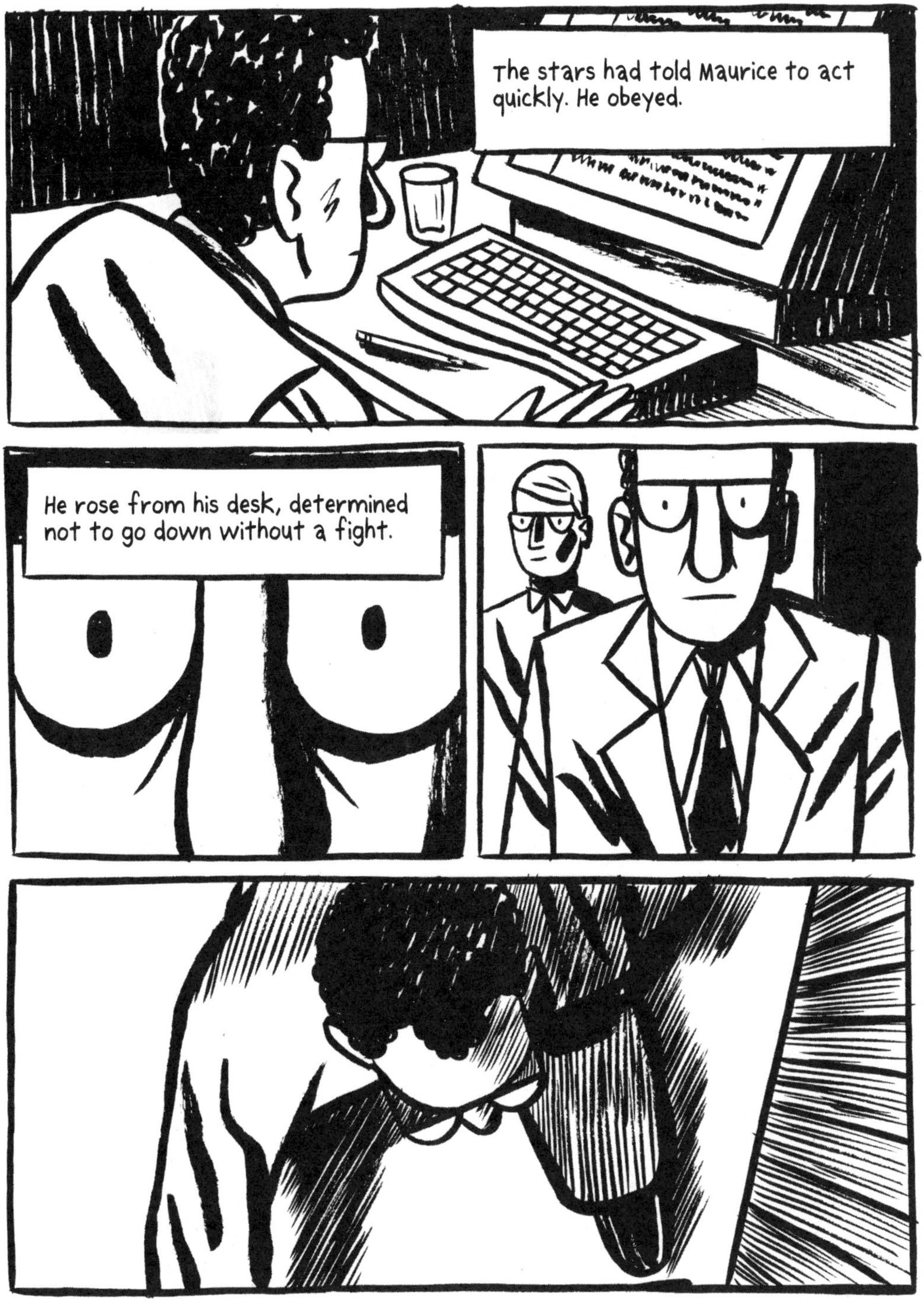
The stars had told Maurice to act quickly. He obeyed.
He rose from his desk, determined not to go down without a fight.

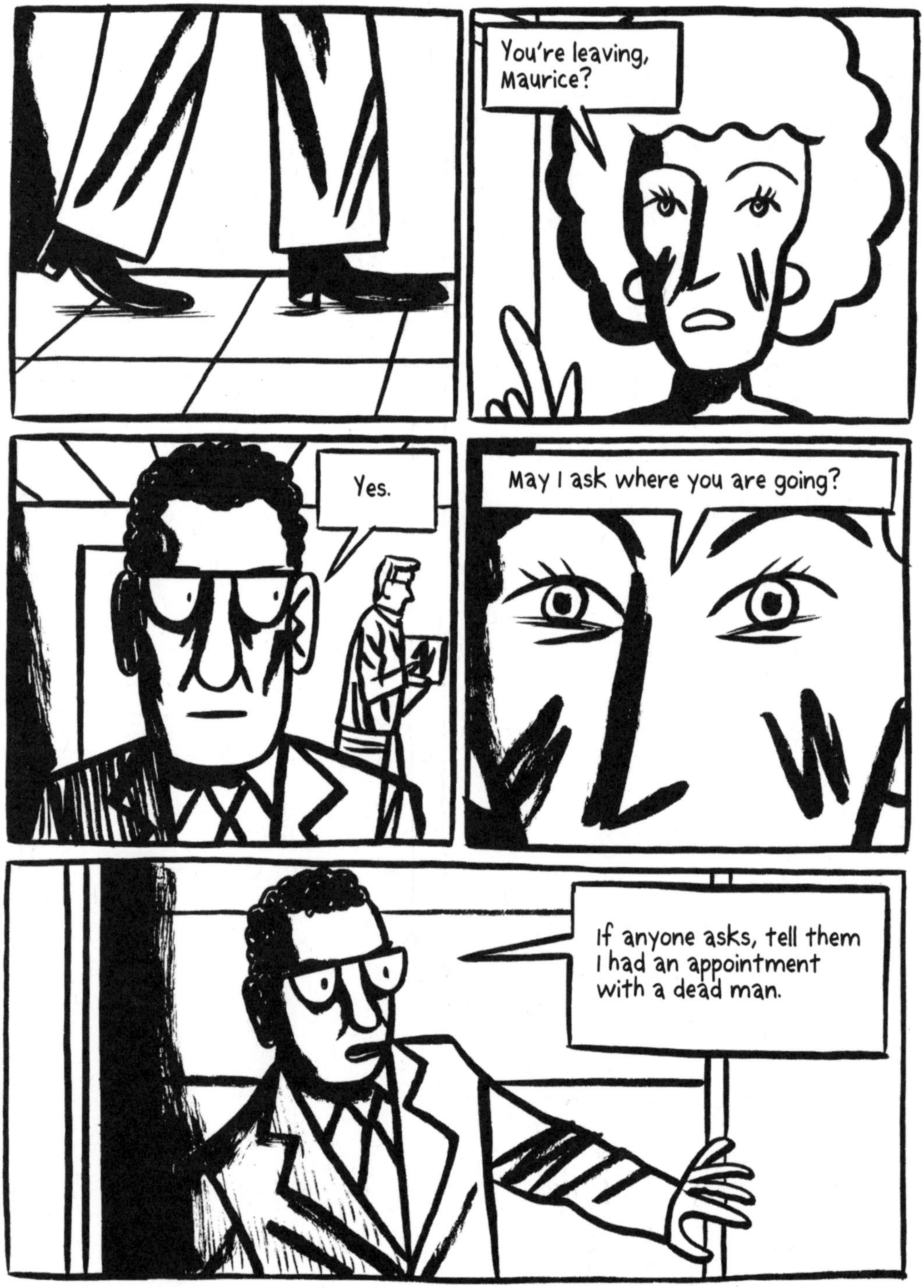
You're leaving, Maurice?
Yes.
May I ask where you are going?
If anyone asks, tell them I had an appointment with a dead man.

# Chapter 2

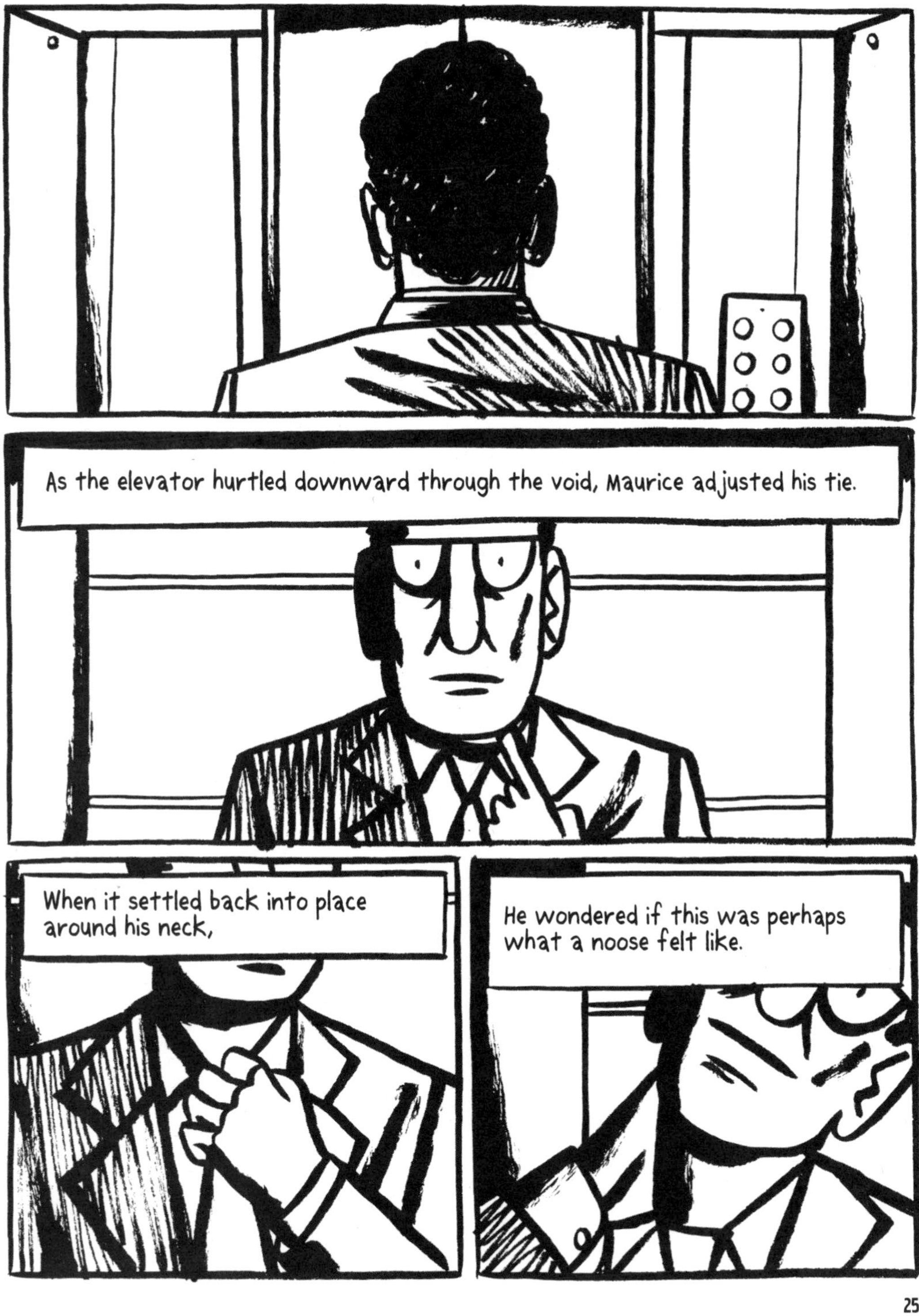
As the elevator hurtled downward through the void, Maurice adjusted his tie.
When it settled back into place around his neck,
He wondered if this was perhaps what a noose felt like.

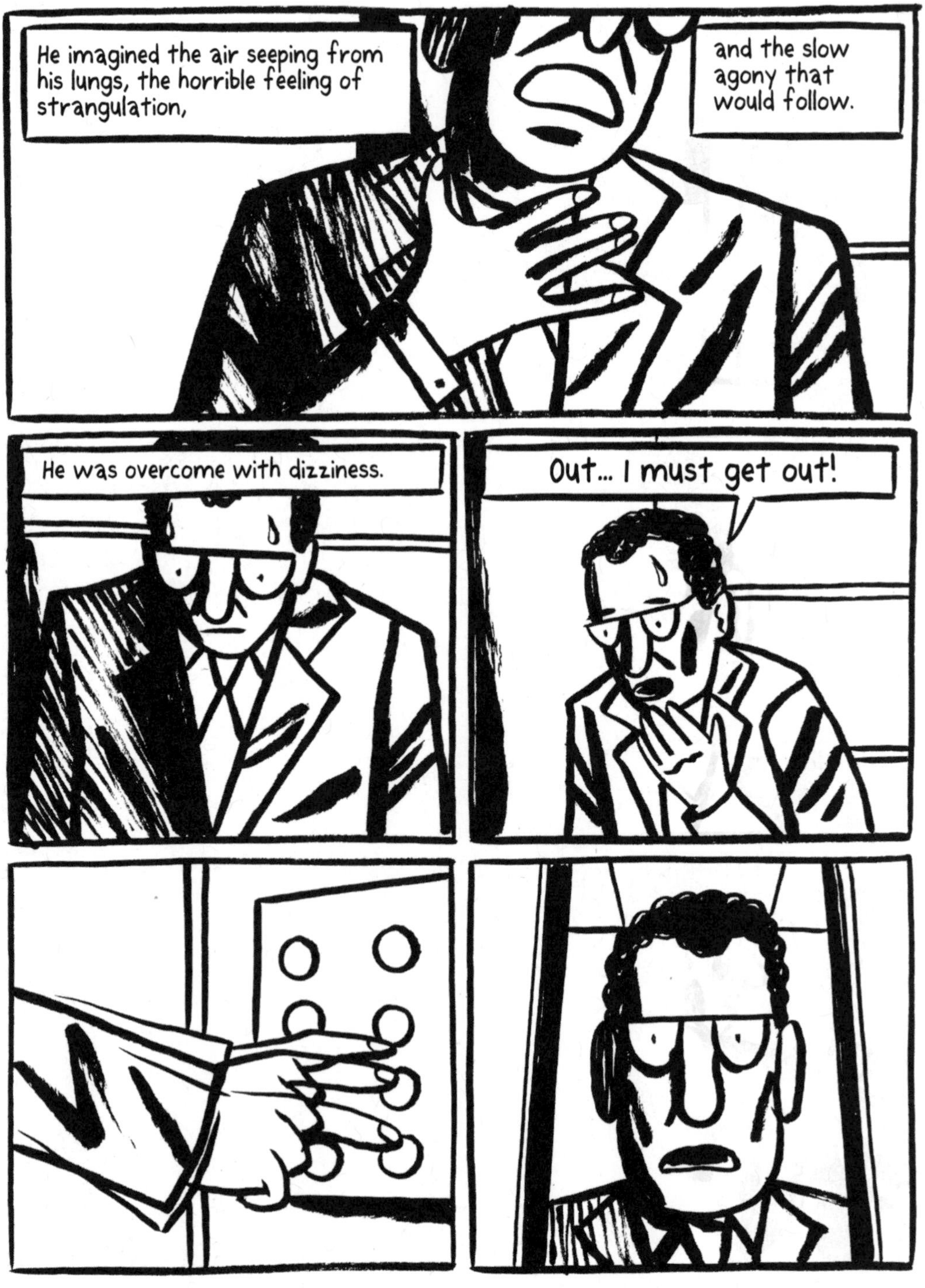
He imagined the air seeping from his lungs, the horrible feeling of strangulation,
and the slow agony that would follow.
He was overcome with dizziness.
Out... I must get out!

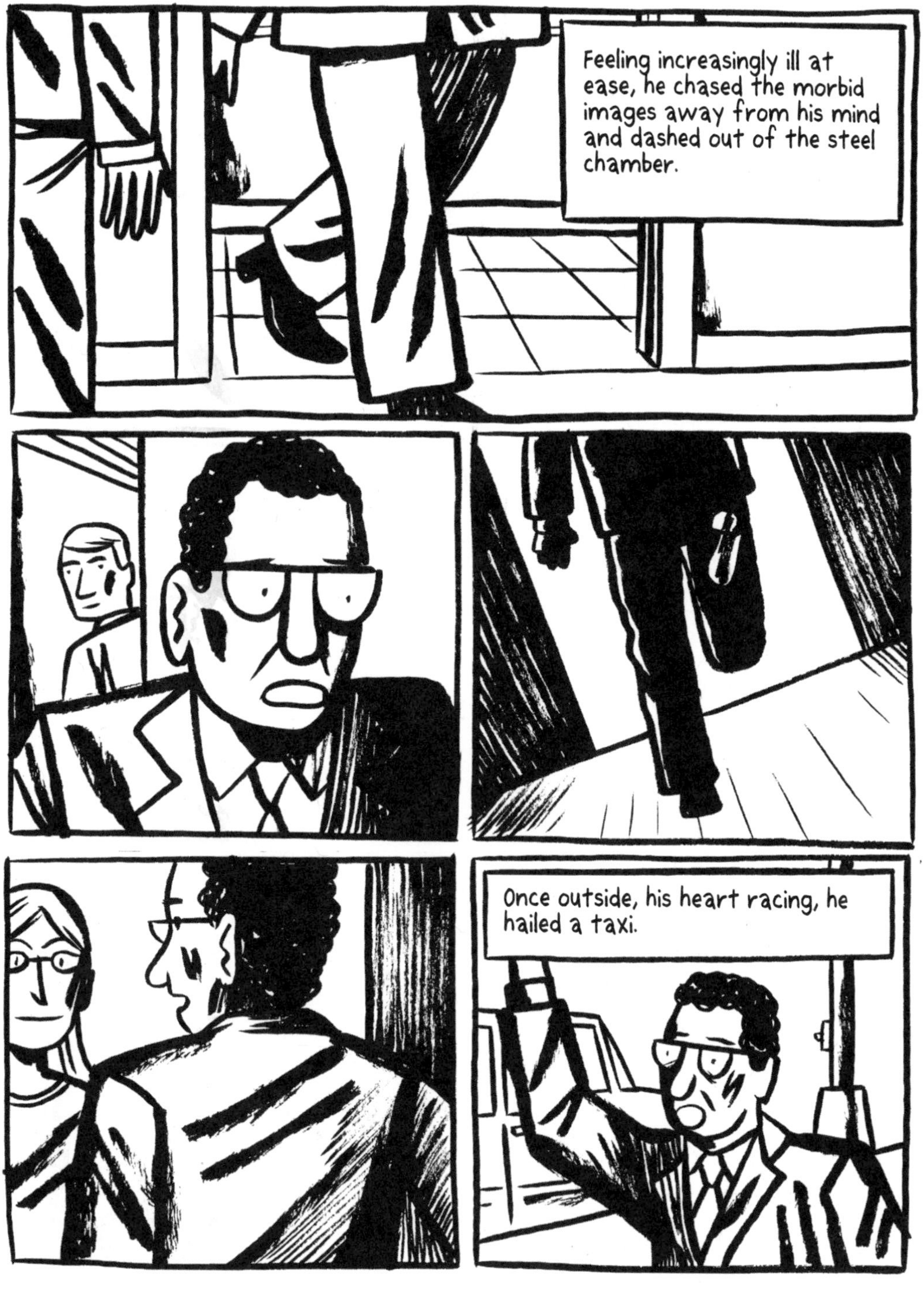
Feeling increasingly ill at ease, he chased the morbid images away from his mind and dashed out of the steel chamber.
Once outside, his heart racing, he hailed a taxi.

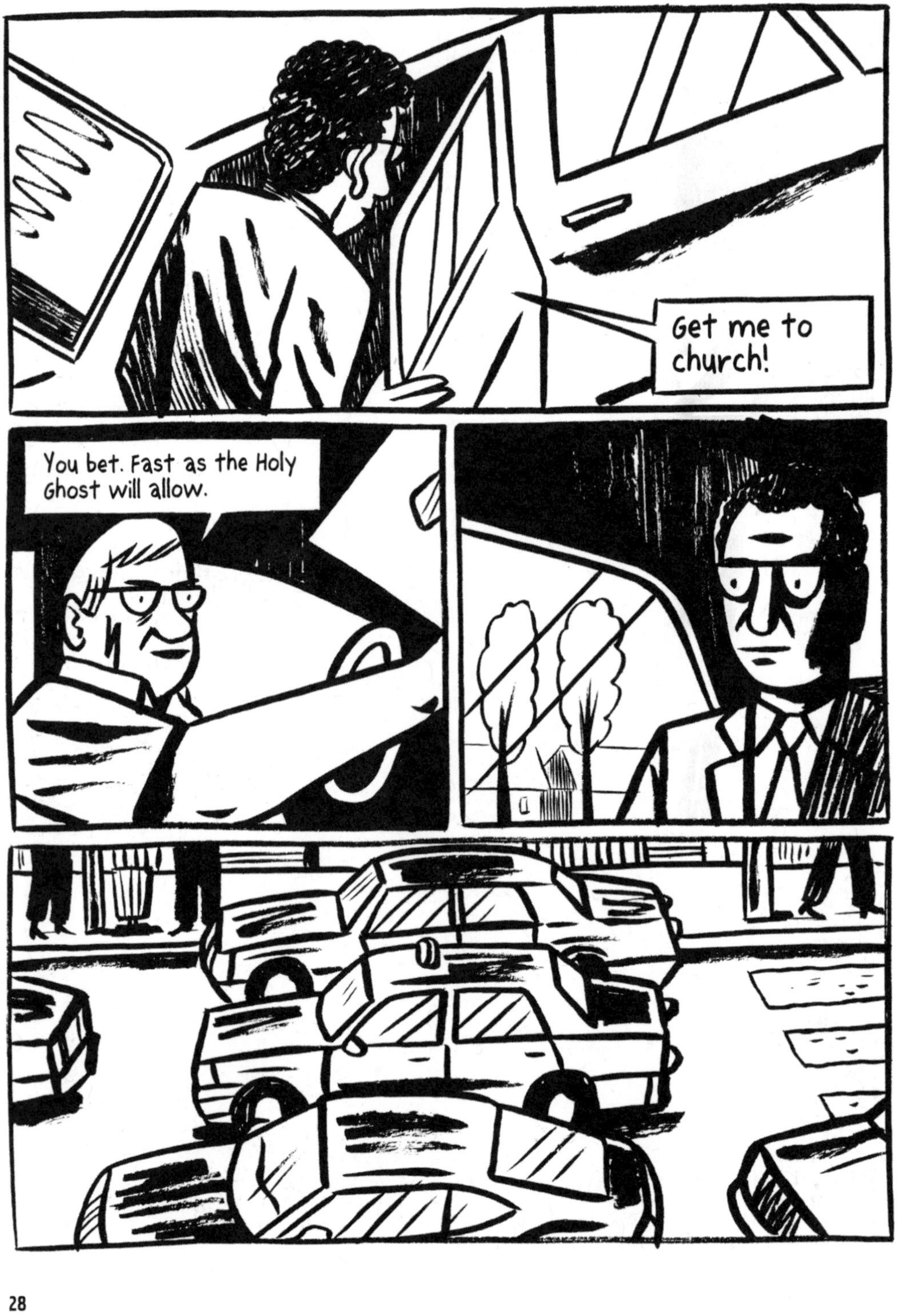
Get me to church!
You bet. Fast as the Holy Ghost will allow.

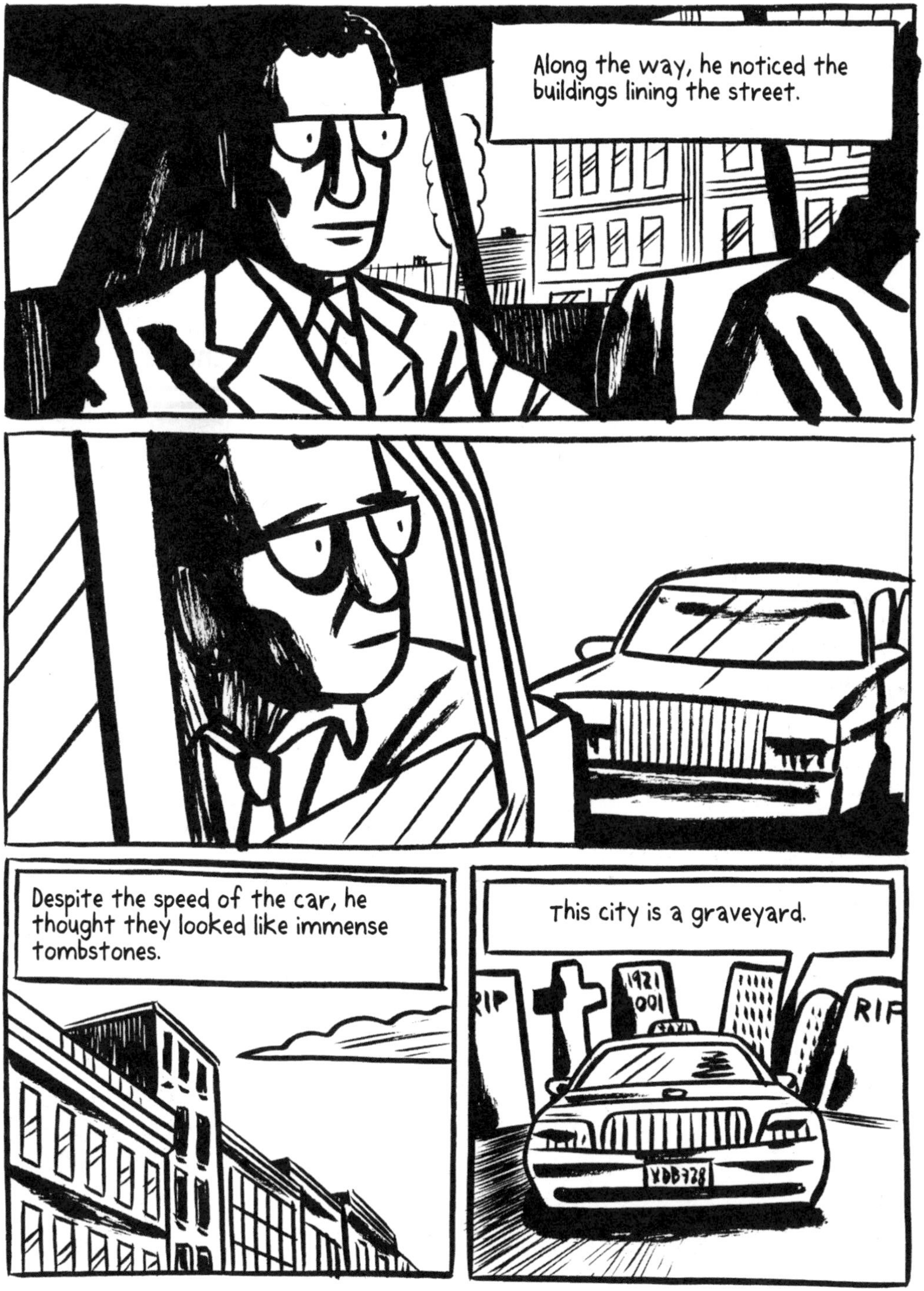
Along the way, he noticed the buildings lining the street.
Despite the speed of the car, he thought they looked like immense tombstones.
This city is a graveyard.
RIP

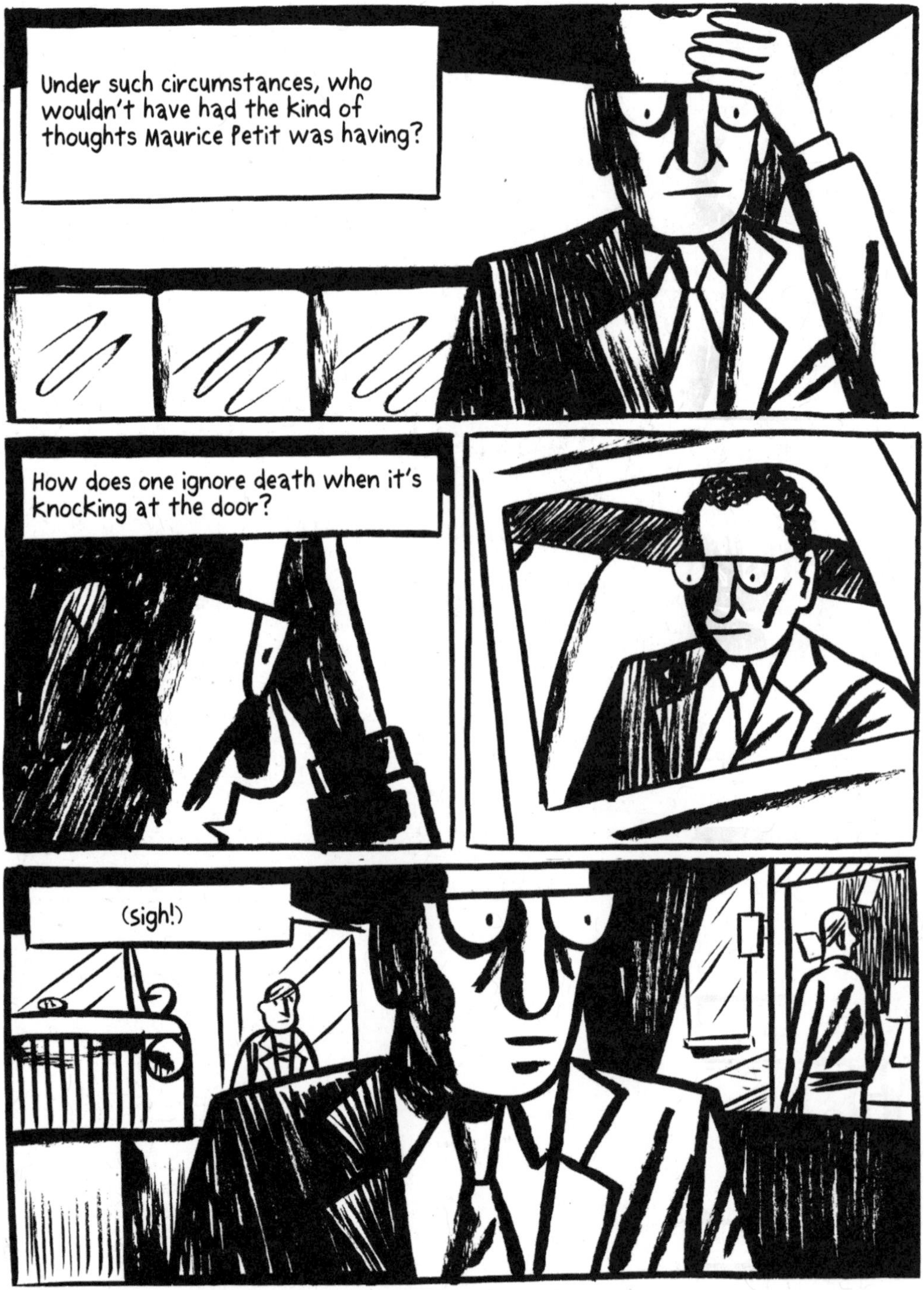

Under such circumstances, who wouldn't have had the kind of thoughts Maurice Petit was having?
How does one ignore death when it's knocking at the door?
(sigh!)

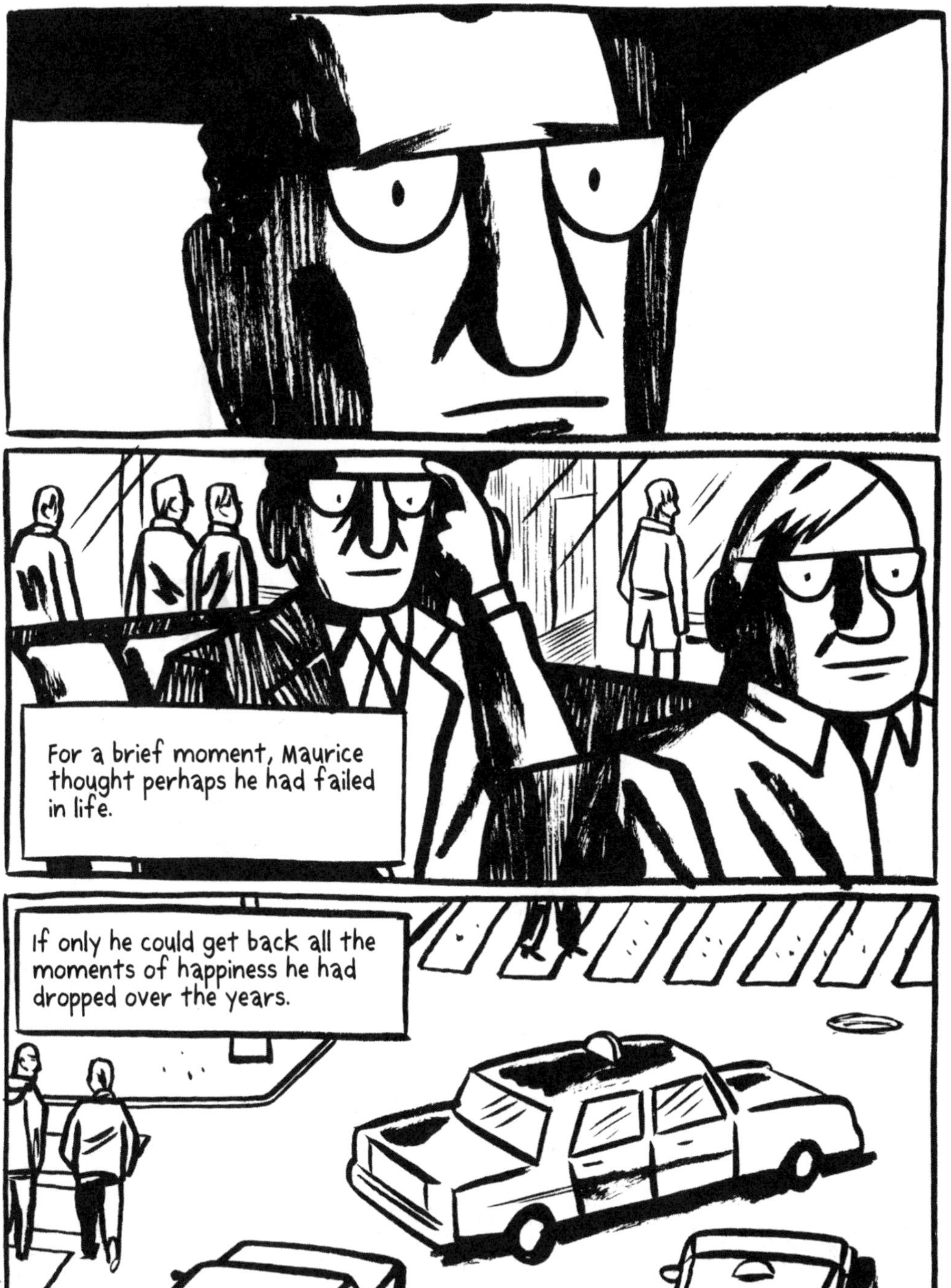

For a brief moment, Maurice thought perhaps he had failed in life.
If only he could get back all the moments of happiness he had dropped over the years.

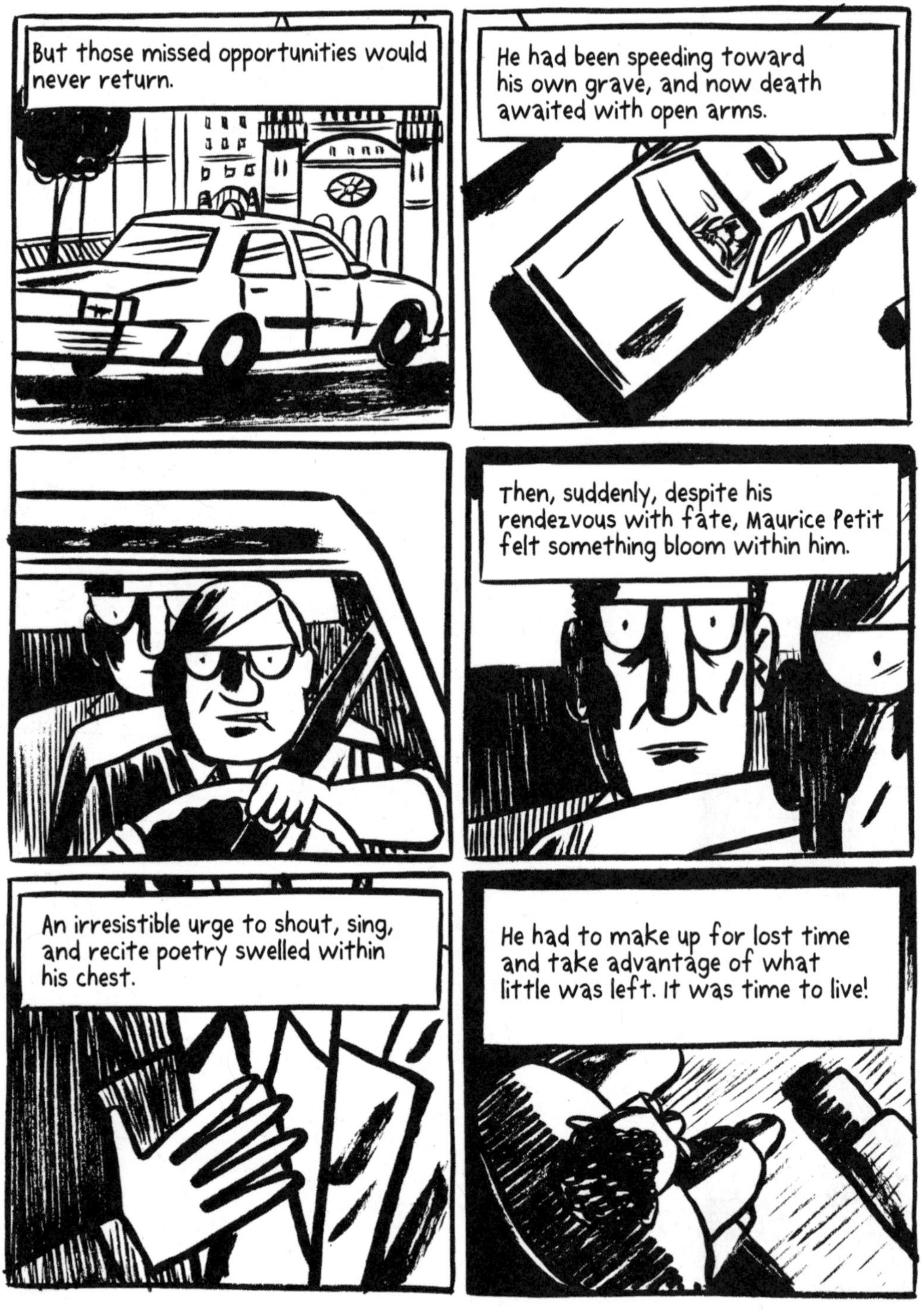
But those missed opportunities would never return.
He had been speeding toward his own grave, and now death awaited with open arms.
Then, suddenly, despite his rendezvous with fate, Maurice Petit felt something bloom within him.
An irresistible urge to shout, sing, and recite poetry swelled within his chest.
He had to make up for lost time and take advantage of what little was left. It was time to live!

The taxi dropped him off in front of the basilica.

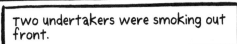

Two undertakers were smoking out front.

It was strange to see these two men, employed by the grim reaper and toying with death the way some will sleep with the boss's wife.

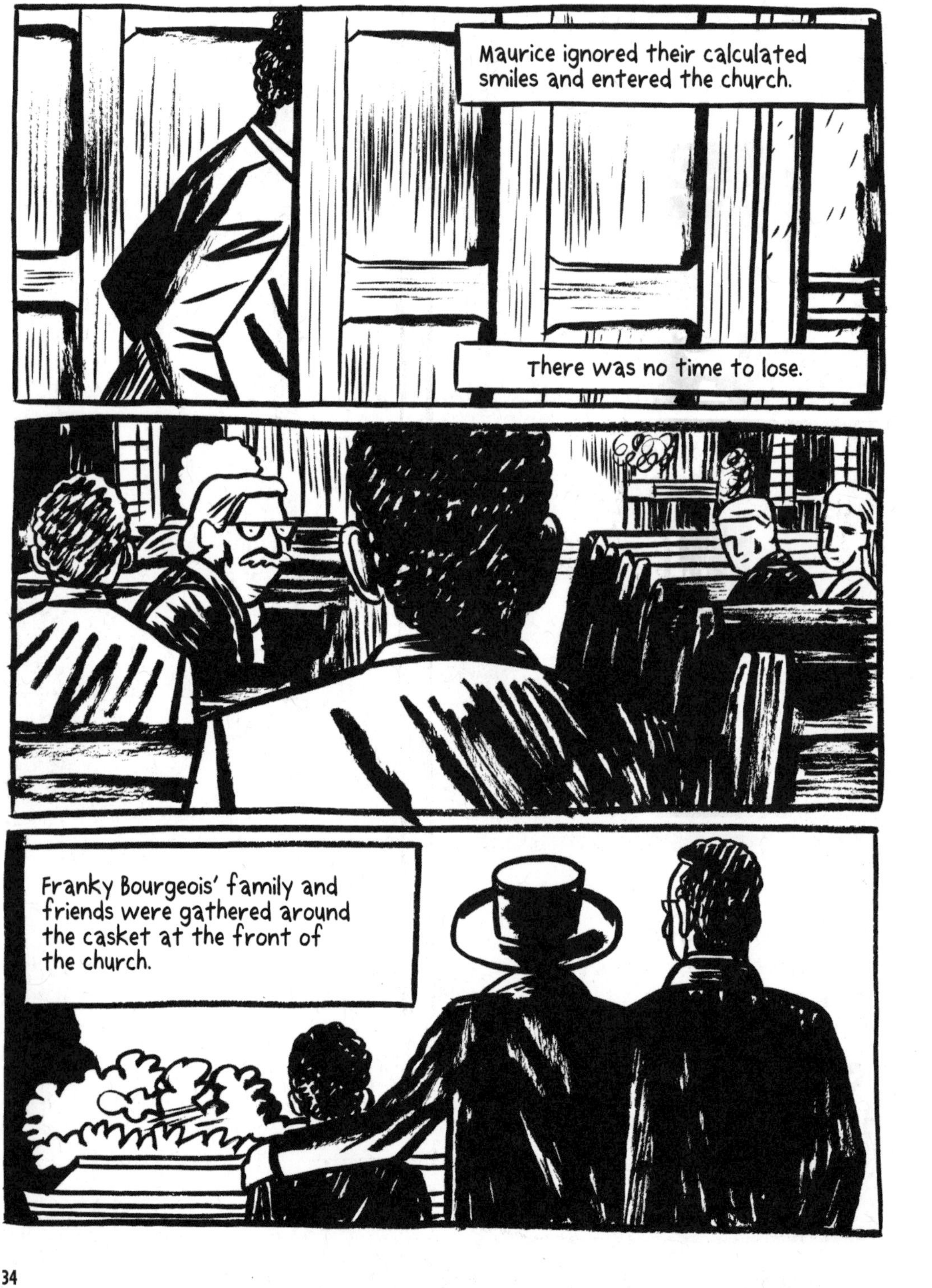
Maurice ignored their calculated smiles and entered the church.
There was no time to lose.
Franky Bourgeois' family and friends were gathered around the casket at the front of the church.

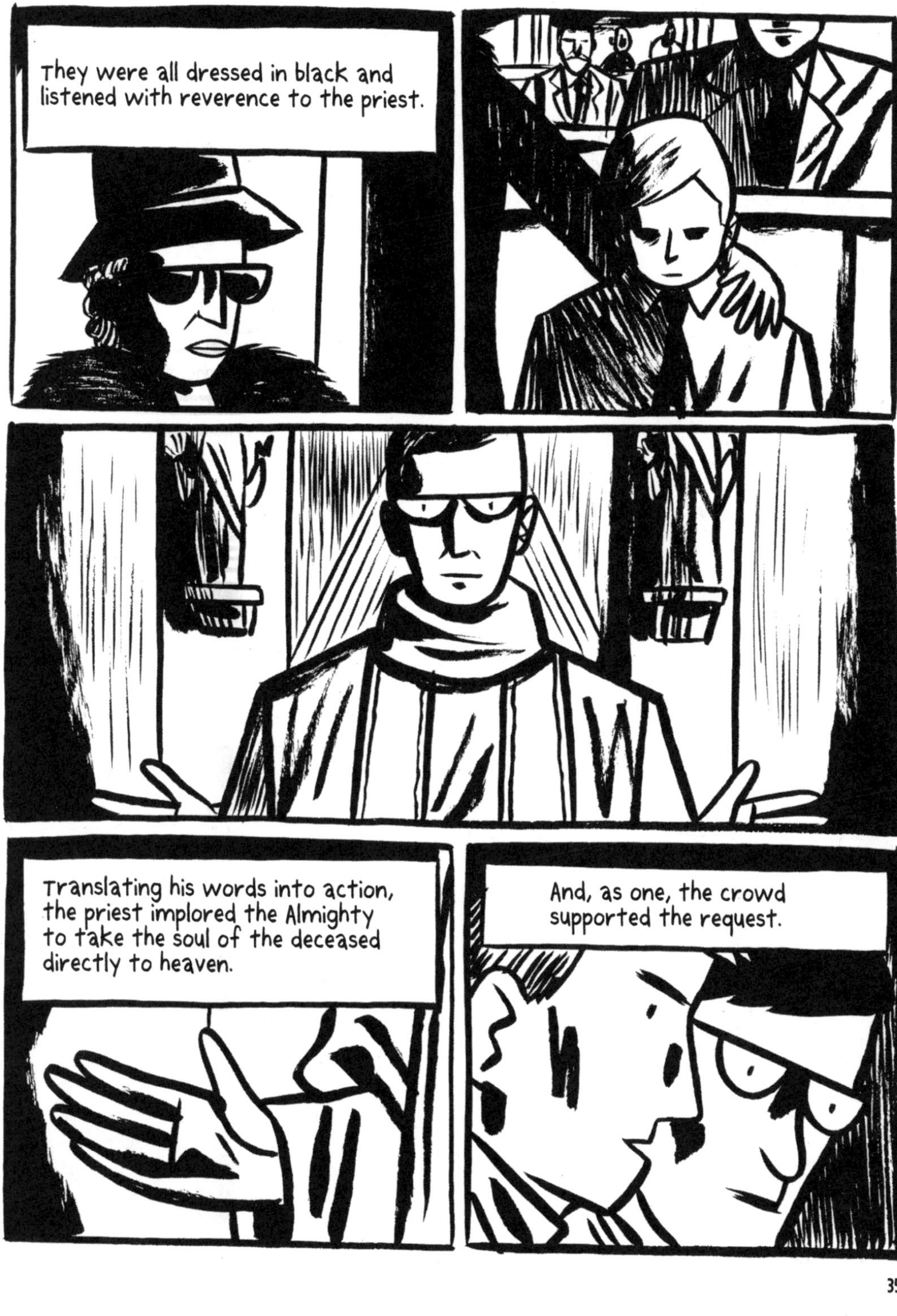
They were all dressed in black and listened with reverence to the priest.
Translating his words into action, the priest implored the Almighty to take the soul of the deceased directly to heaven.
And, as one, the crowd supported the request.

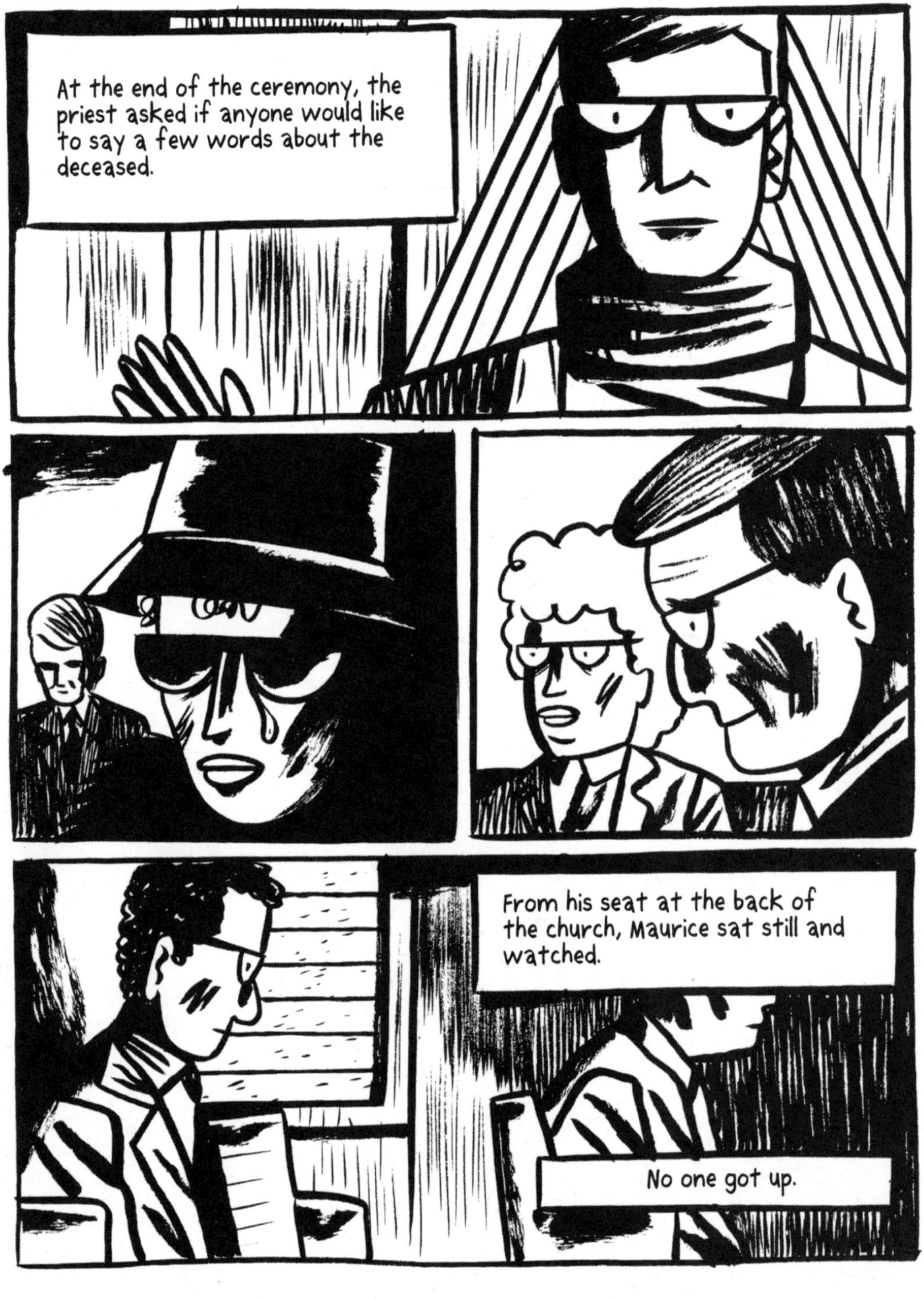
At the end of the ceremony, the priest asked if anyone would like to say a few words about the deceased.
From his seat at the back of the church, Maurice sat still and watched.
No one got up.

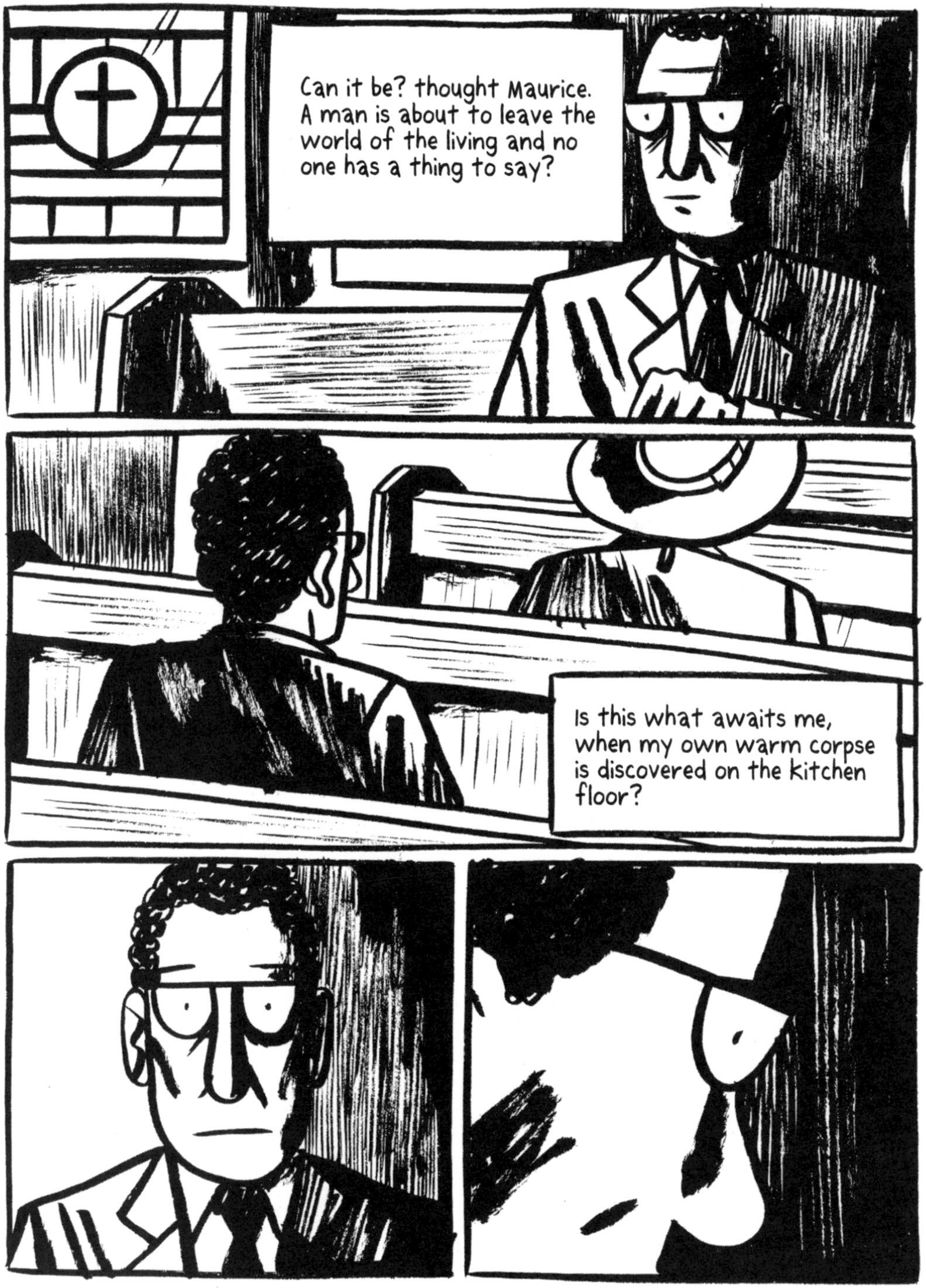
Can it be? thought Maurice. A man is about to leave the world of the living and no one has a thing to say?
Is this what awaits me, when my own warm corpse is discovered on the kitchen floor?

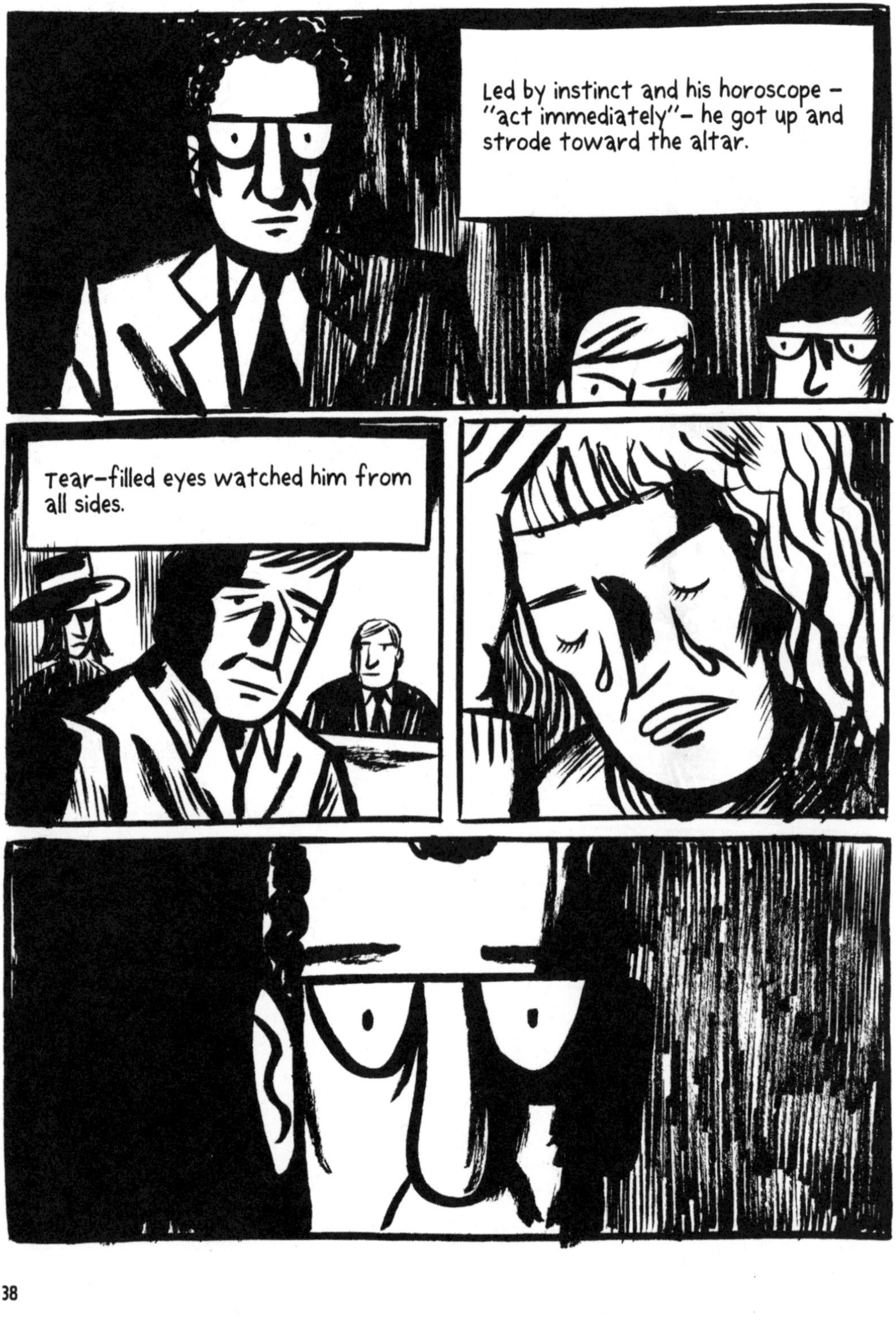
Led by instinct and his horoscope – "act immediately"– he got up and strode toward the altar.
Tear–filled eyes watched him from all sides.

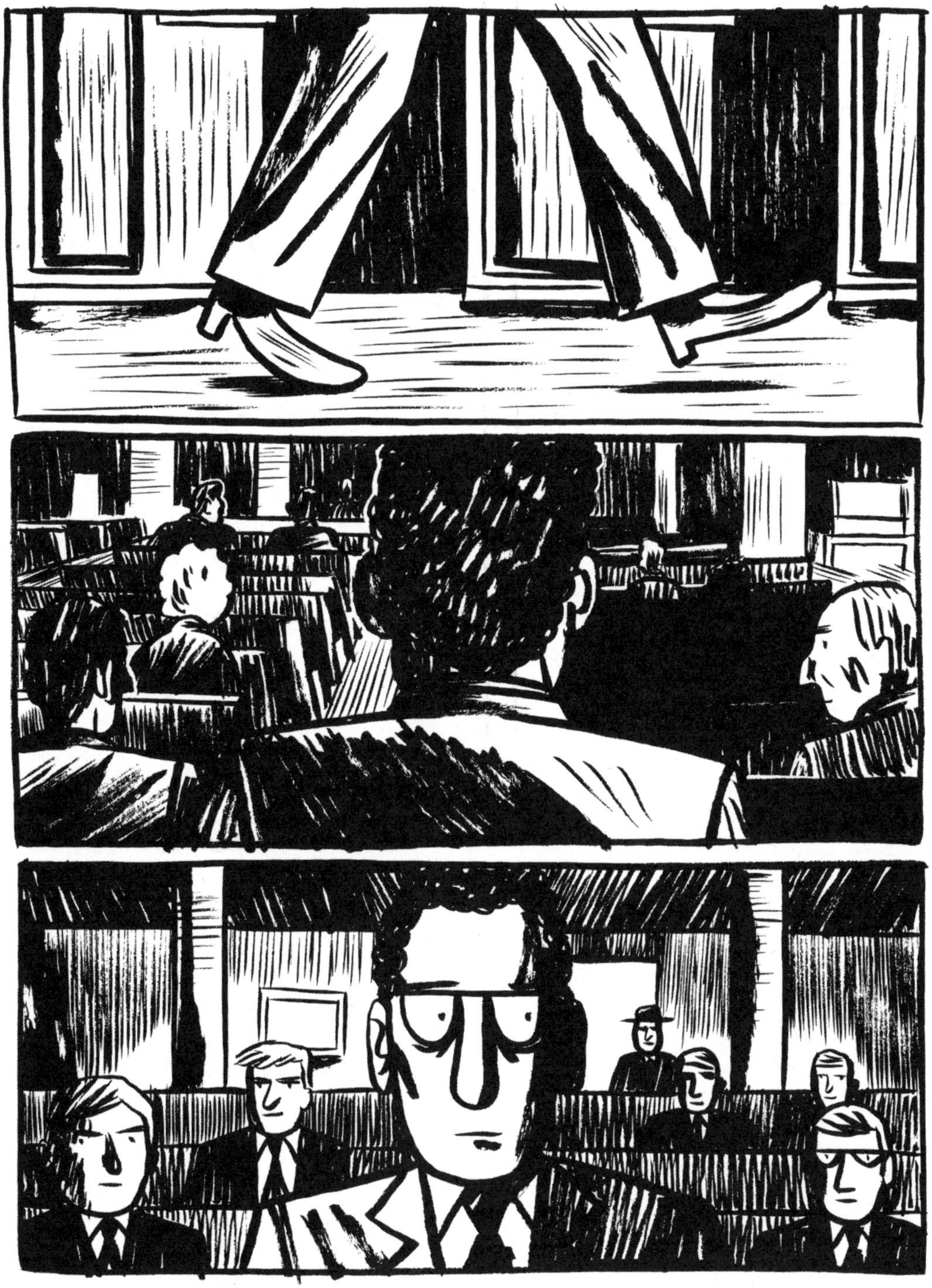

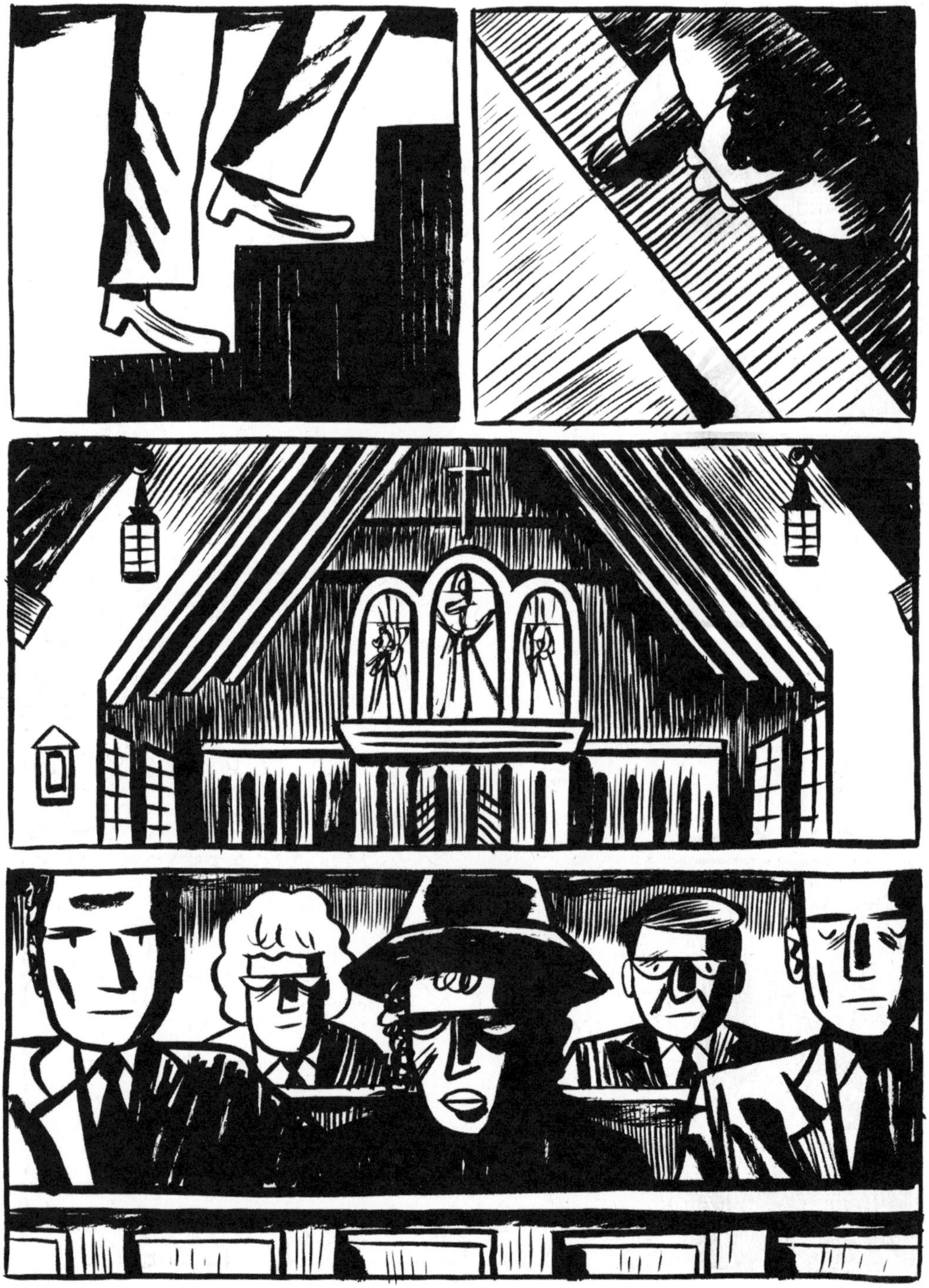

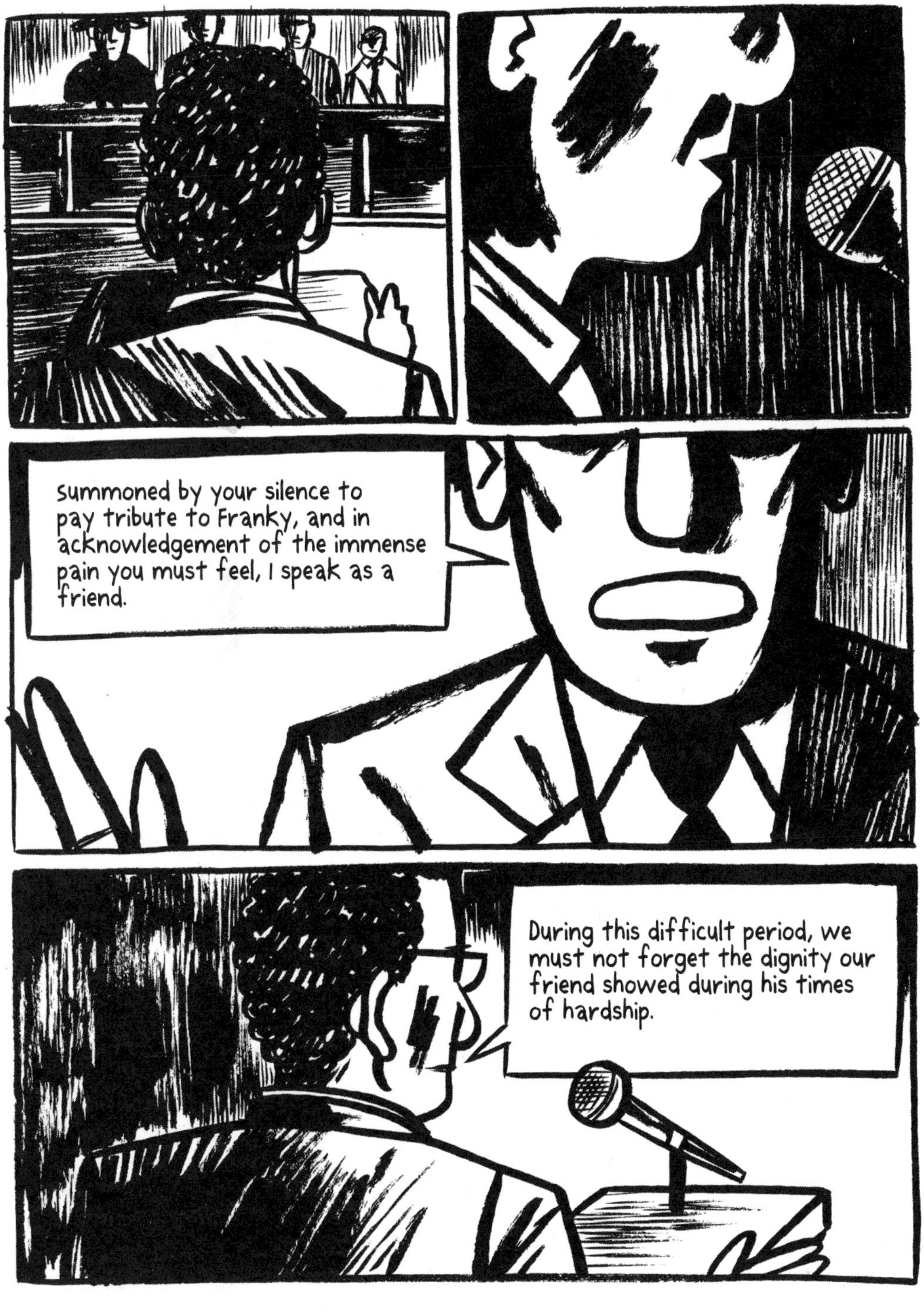
summoned by your silence to pay tribute to Franky, and in acknowledgement of the immense pain you must feel, I speak as a friend.
During this difficult period, we must not forget the dignity our friend showed during his times of hardship.

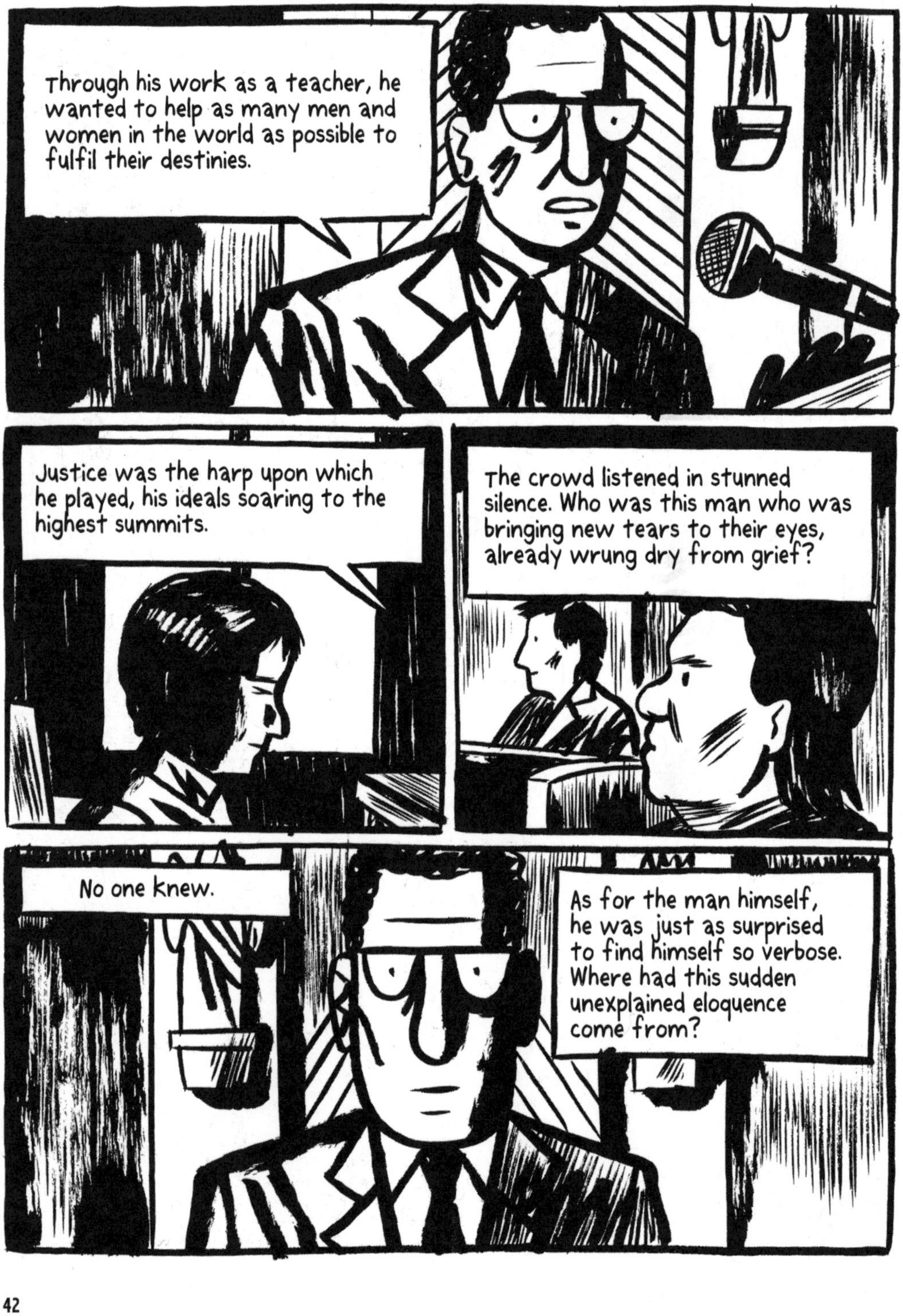
Through his work as a teacher, he wanted to help as many men and women in the world as possible to fulfil their destinies.
Justice was the harp upon which he played, his ideals soaring to the highest summits.
The crowd listened in stunned silence. Who was this man who was bringing new tears to their eyes, already wrung dry from grief?
No one knew.
As for the man himself, he was just as surprised to find himself so verbose. Where had this sudden unexplained eloquence come from?

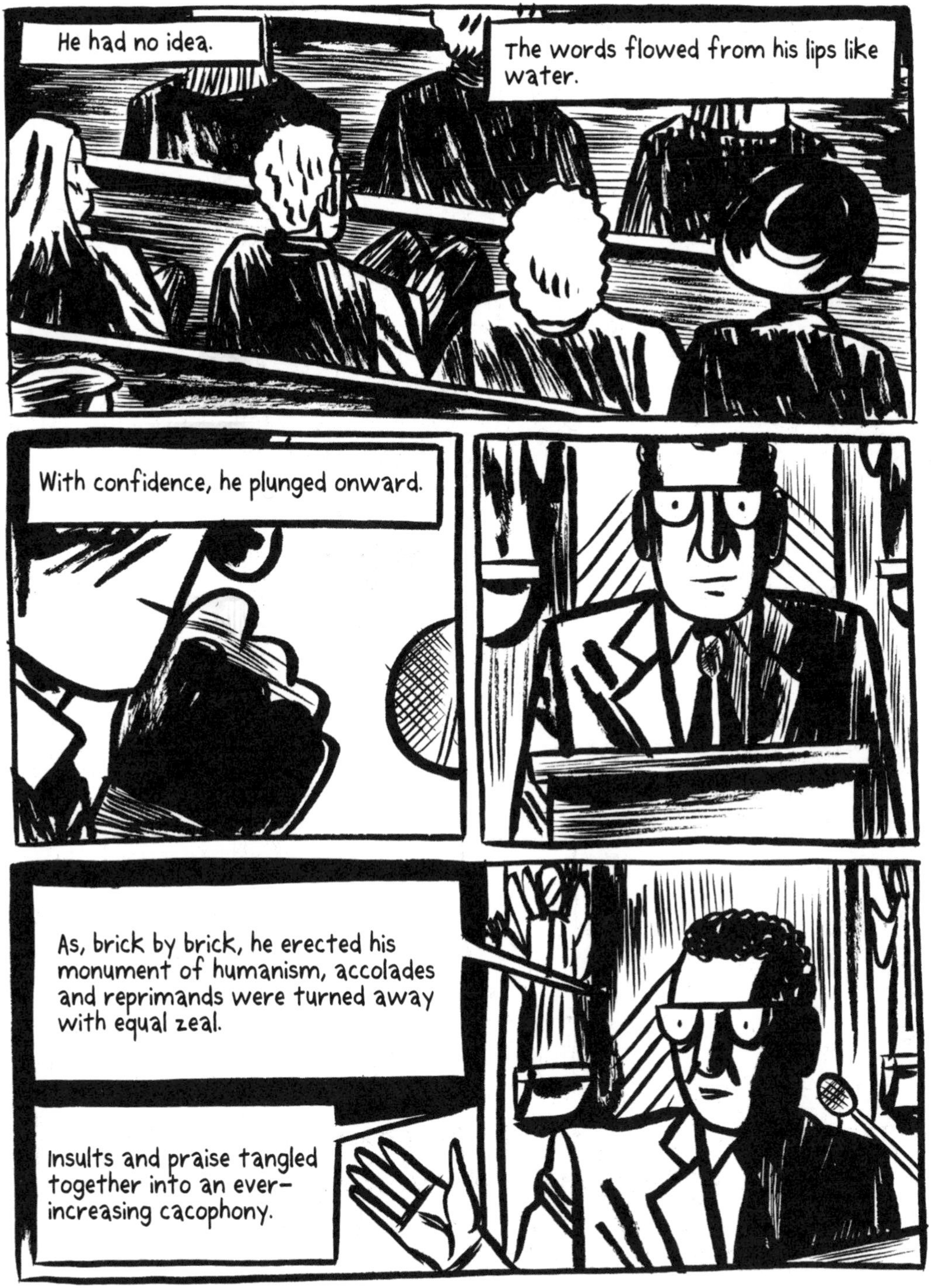
He had no idea.
The words flowed from his lips like water.
With confidence, he plunged onward.
As, brick by brick, he erected his monument of humanism, accolades and reprimands were turned away with equal zeal.
Insults and praise tangled together into an ever-increasing cacophony.

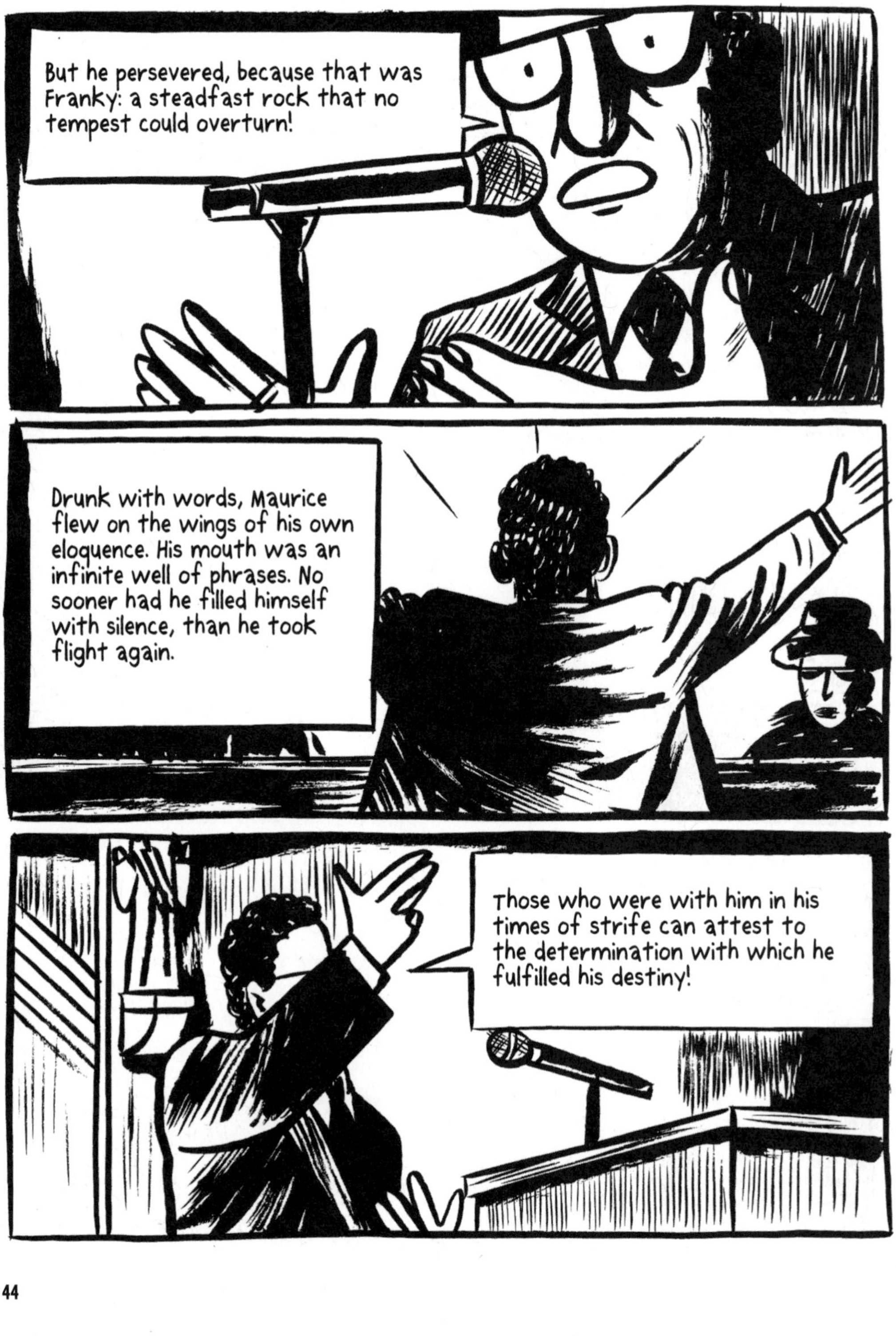
But he persevered, because that was Franky: a steadfast rock that no tempest could overturn!
Drunk with words, Maurice flew on the wings of his own eloquence. His mouth was an infinite well of phrases. No sooner had he filled himself with silence, than he took flight again.
Those who were with him in his times of strife can attest to the determination with which he fulfilled his destiny!

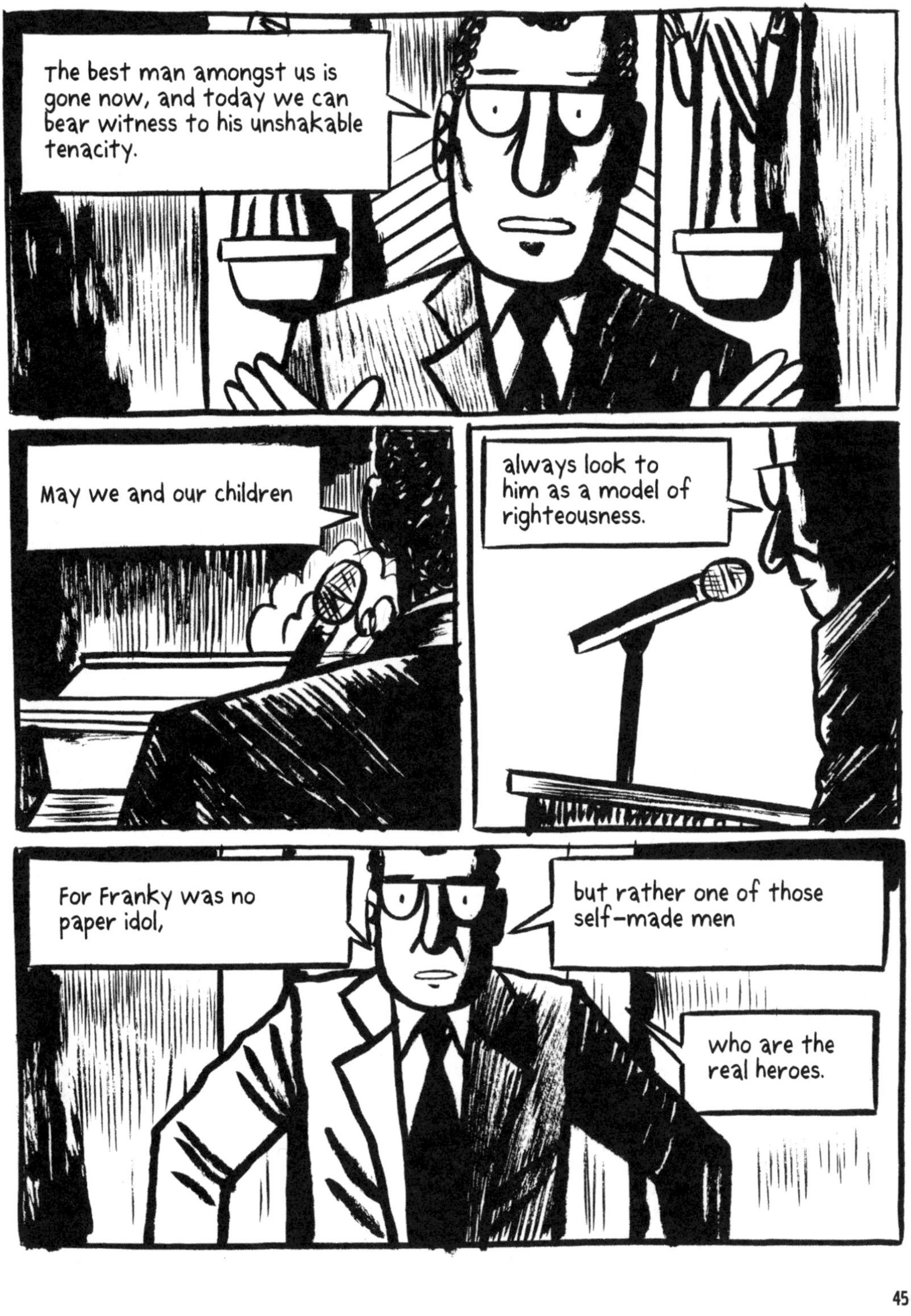
The best man amongst us is gone now, and today we can bear witness to his unshakable tenacity.
May we and our children
always look to him as a model of righteousness.
For Franky was no paper idol,
but rather one of those self-made men
who are the real heroes.

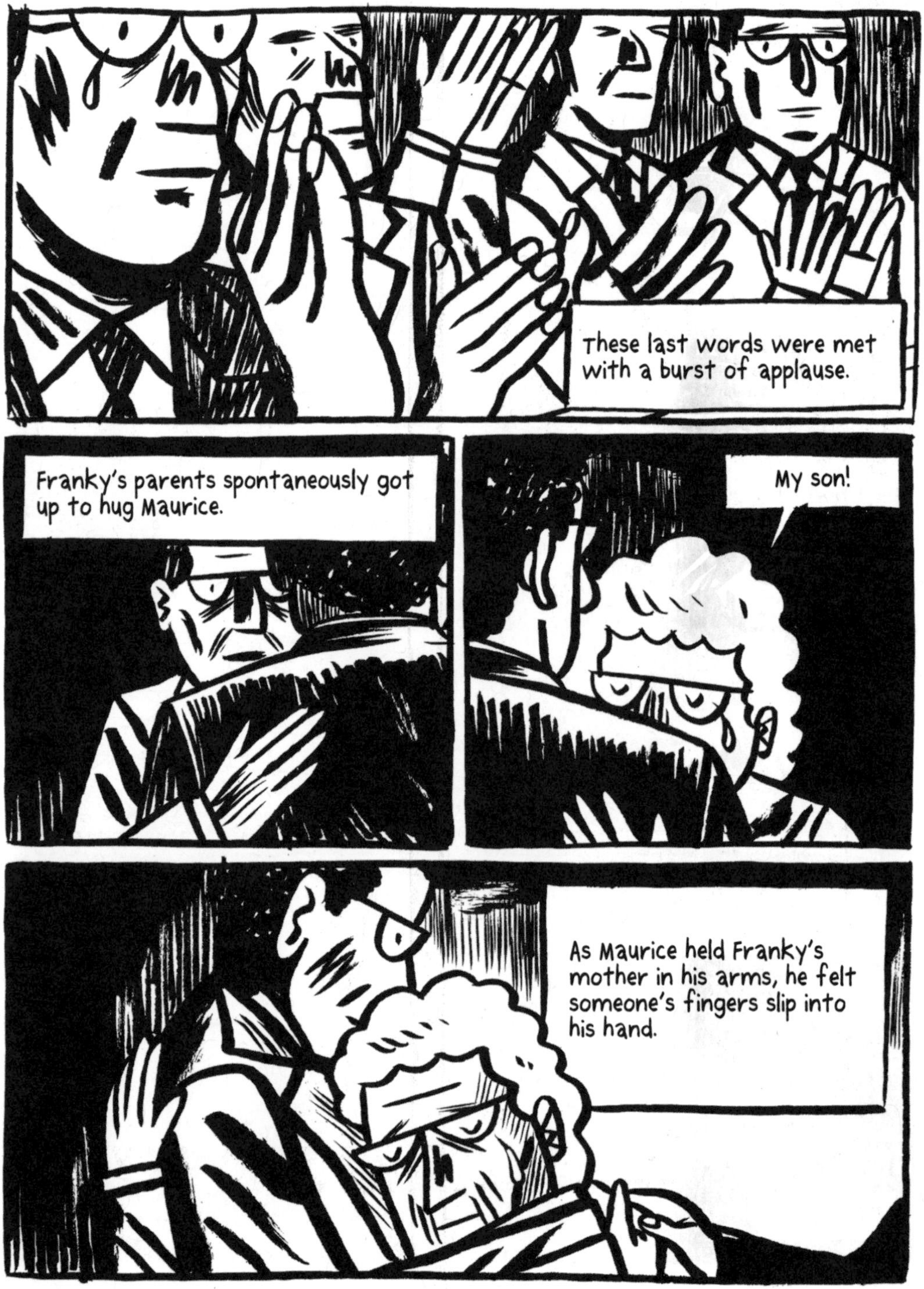
These last words were met with a burst of applause.
Franky's parents spontaneously got up to hug Maurice.
My son!
As Maurice held Franky's mother in his arms, he felt someone's fingers slip into his hand.

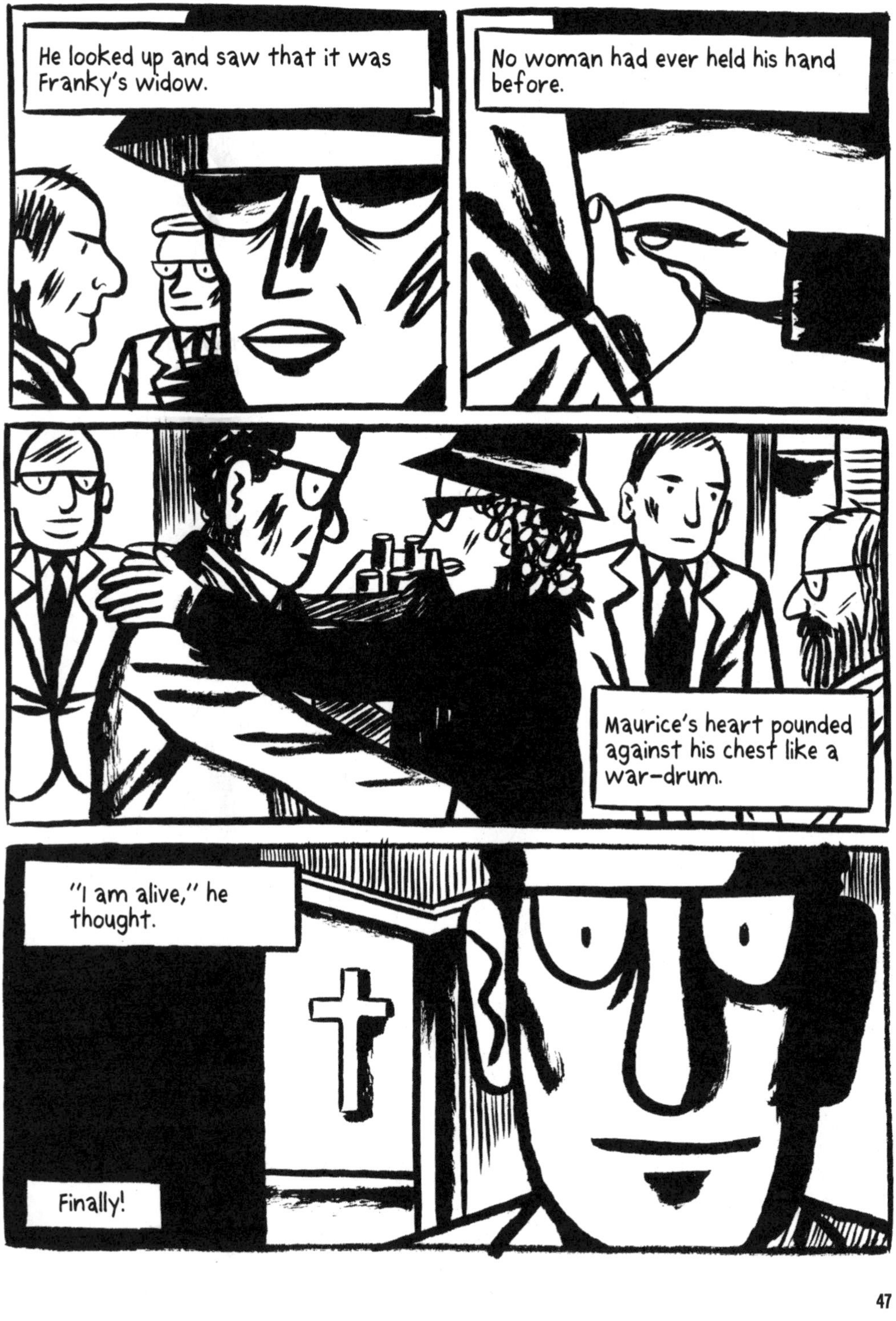
He looked up and saw that it was Franky's widow.
No woman had ever held his hand before.
Maurice's heart pounded against his chest like a war-drum.
"I am alive," he thought.
Finally!

# Chapter 3

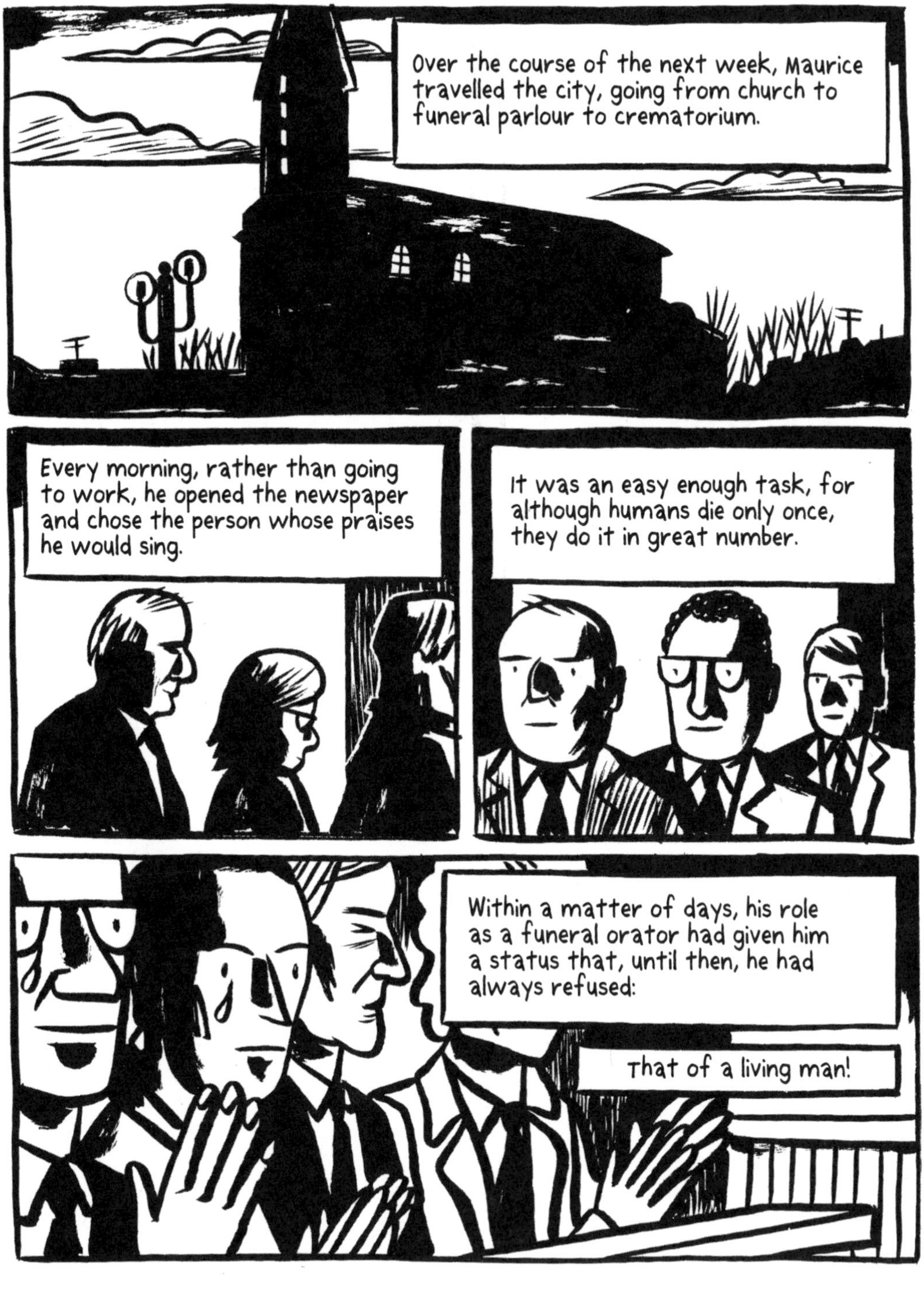
Over the course of the next week, Maurice travelled the city, going from church to funeral parlour to crematorium.
Every morning, rather than going to work, he opened the newspaper and chose the person whose praises he would sing.
It was an easy enough task, for although humans die only once, they do it in great number.
Within a matter of days, his role as a funeral orator had given him a status that, until then, he had always refused:
That of a living man!

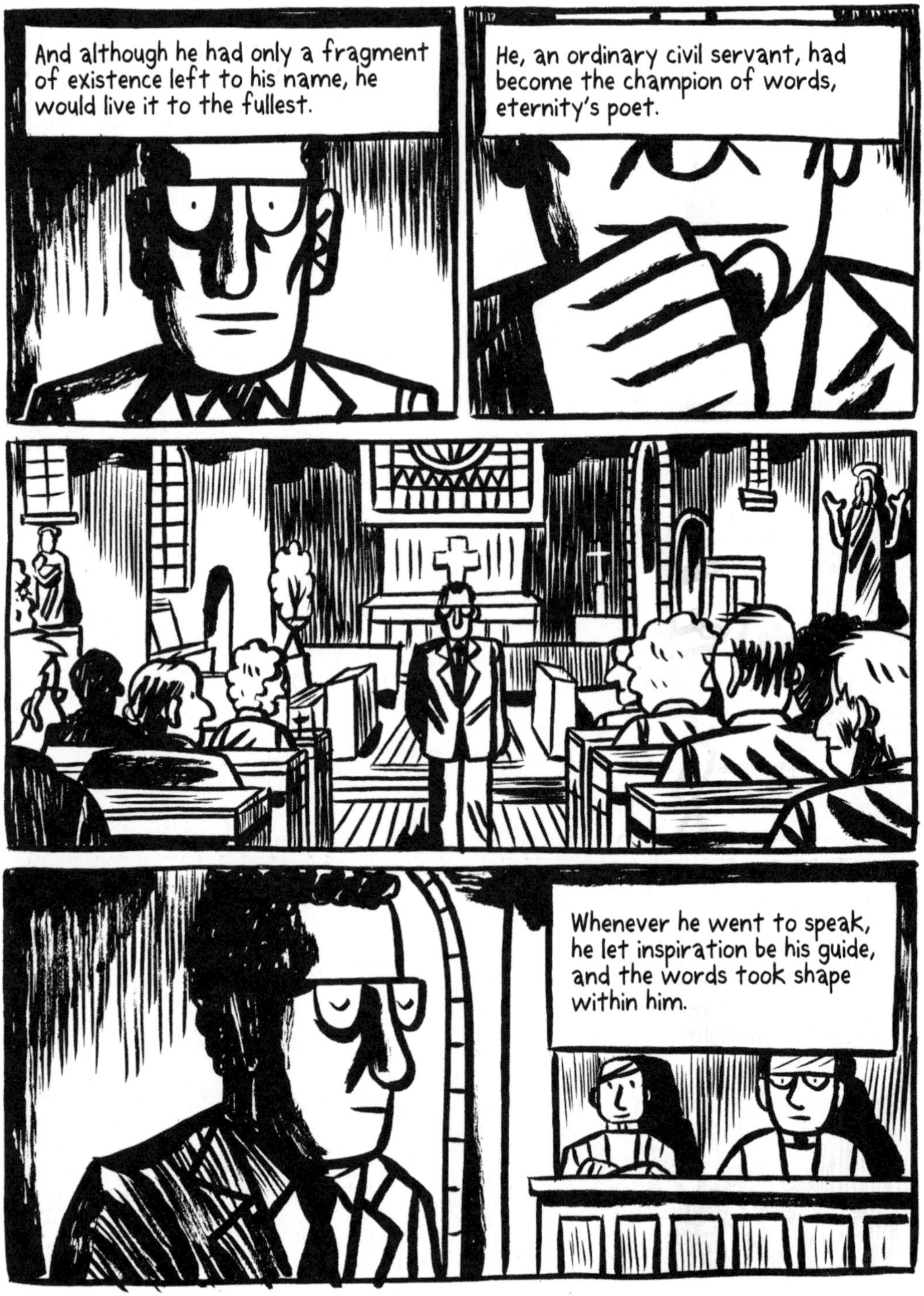
And although he had only a fragment of existence left to his name, he would live it to the fullest.
He, an ordinary civil servant, had become the champion of words, eternity's poet.
Whenever he went to speak, he let inspiration be his guide, and the words took shape within him.

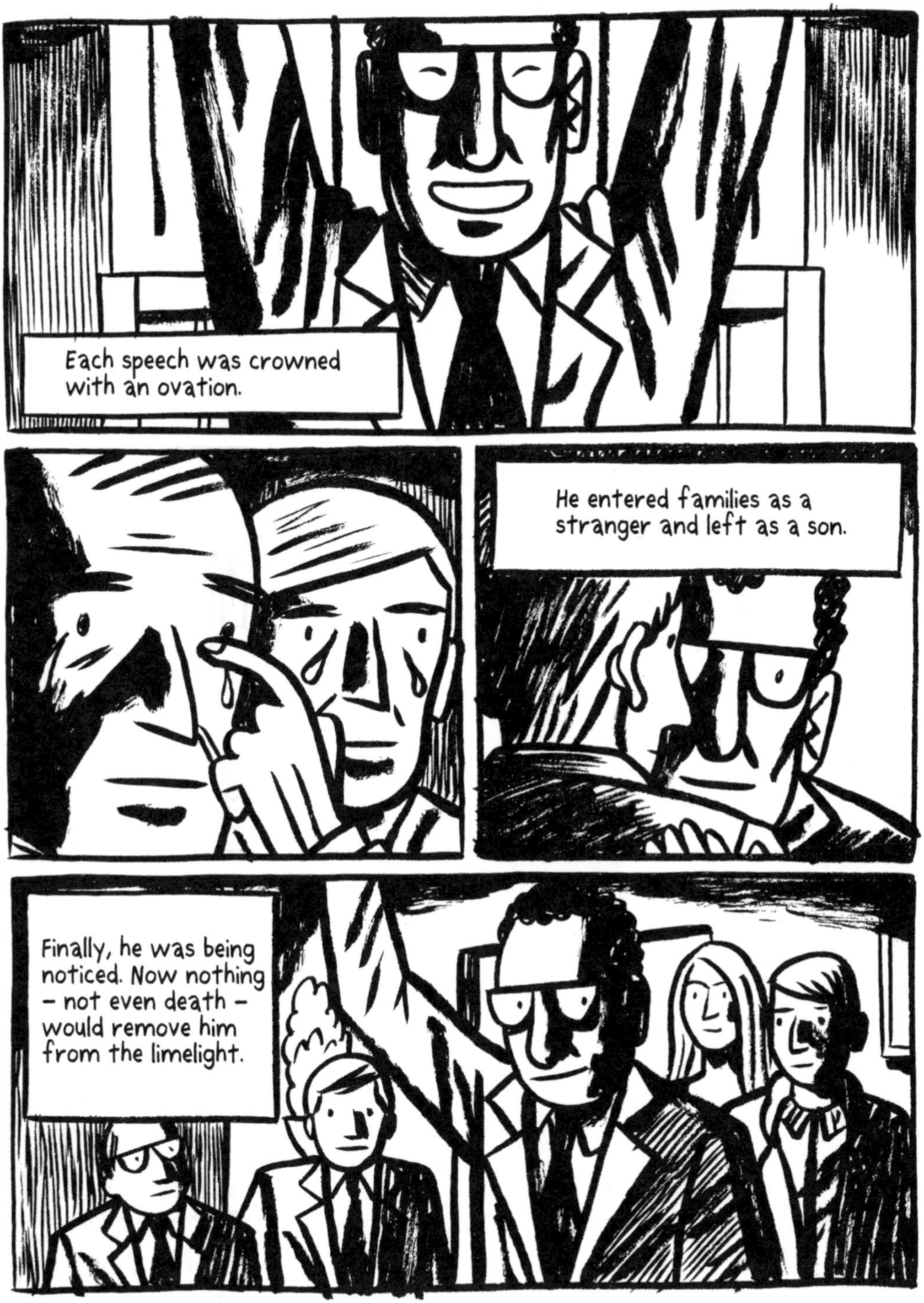
Each speech was crowned with an ovation.
He entered families as a stranger and left as a son.
Finally, he was being noticed. Now nothing – not even death – would remove him from the limelight.

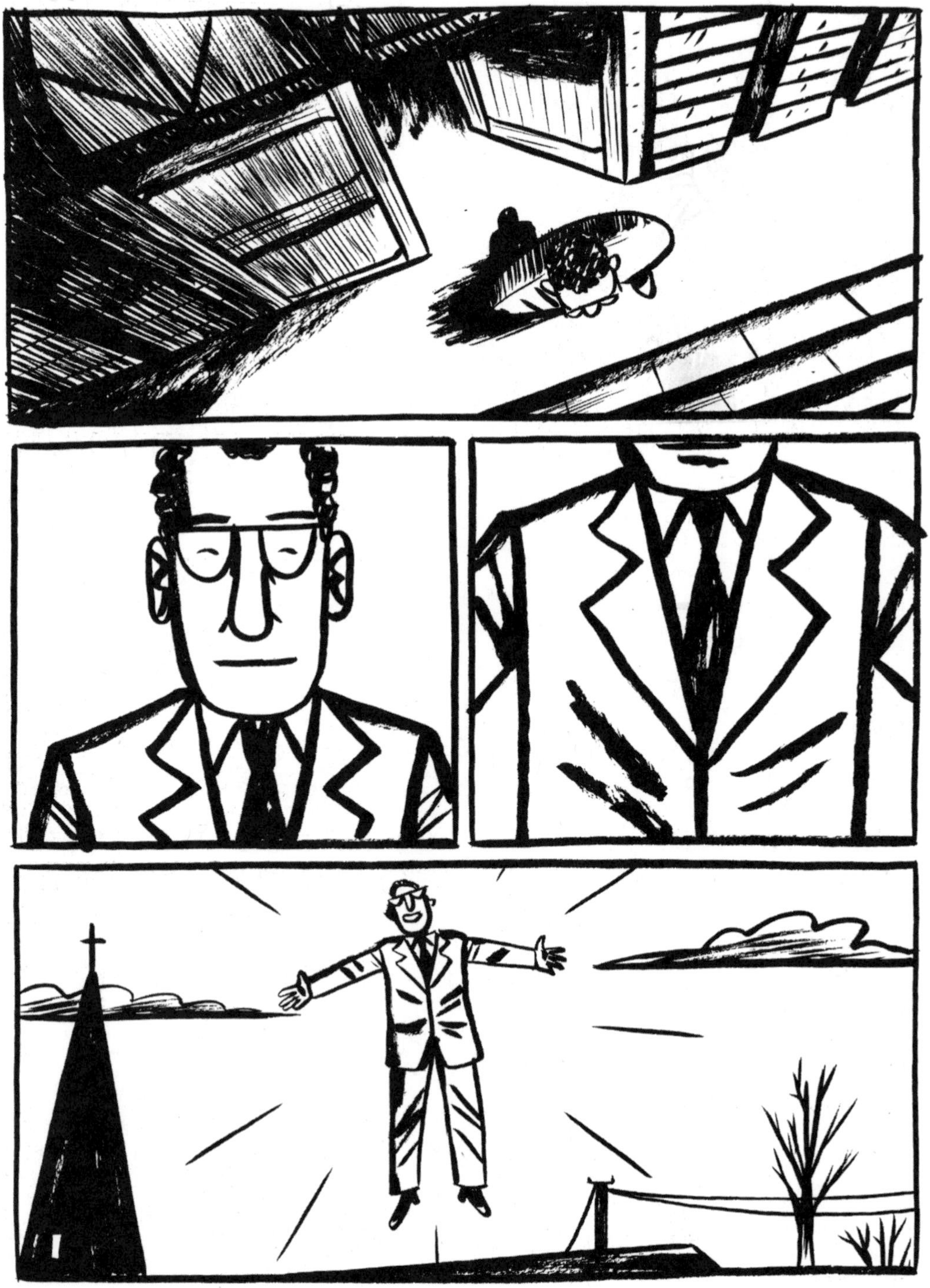

One morning though, something different awaited Maurice.

My father, Albert Breccia, had died in a car accident, and those who wished to pay their last respects had until noon to do so.

The graveyard orator had found his subject for the day.

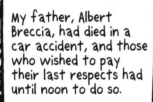

He ate a quick breakfast and hopped on the bus.

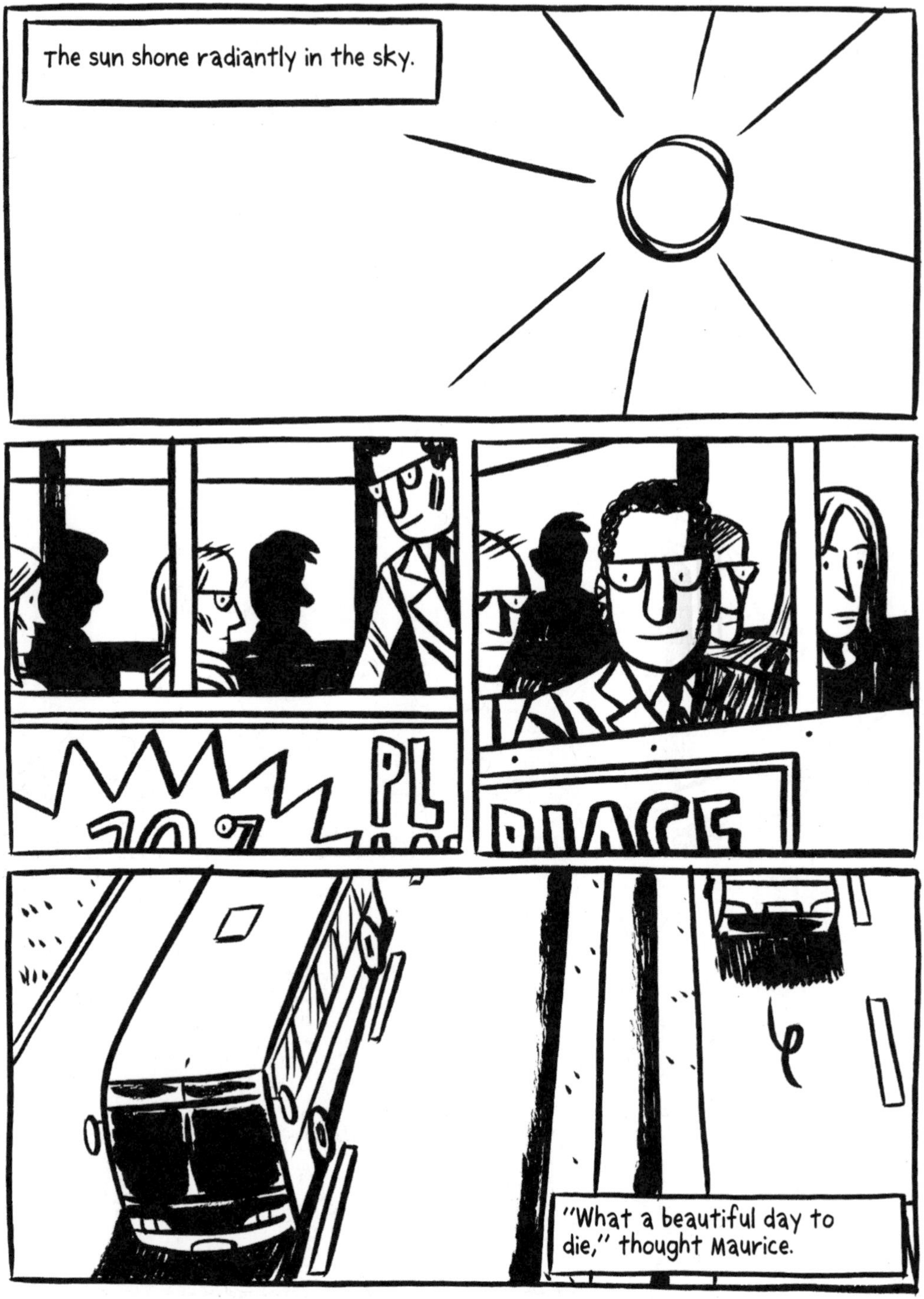
The sun shone radiantly in the sky.
PL
"What a beautiful day to die," thought Maurice.

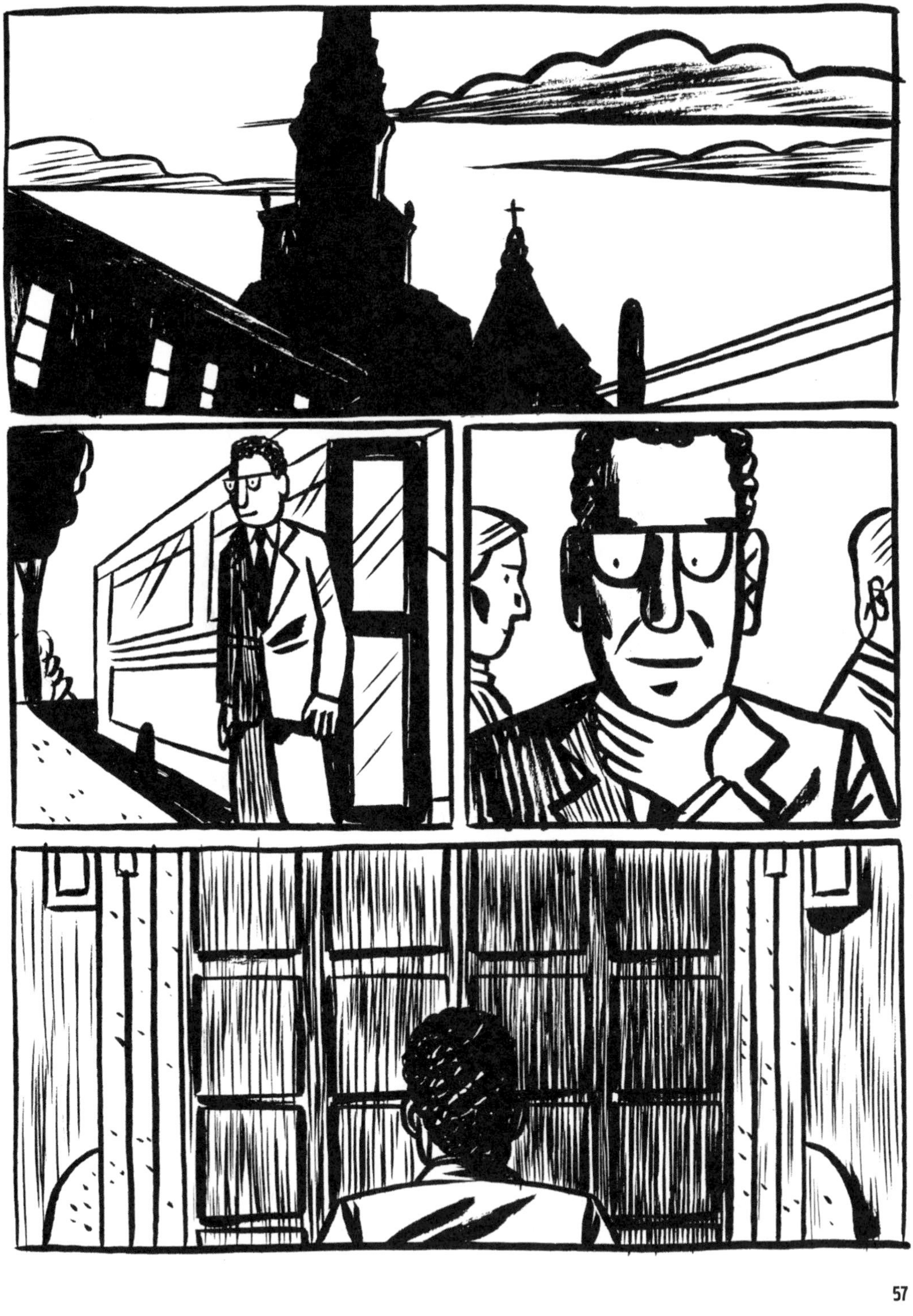

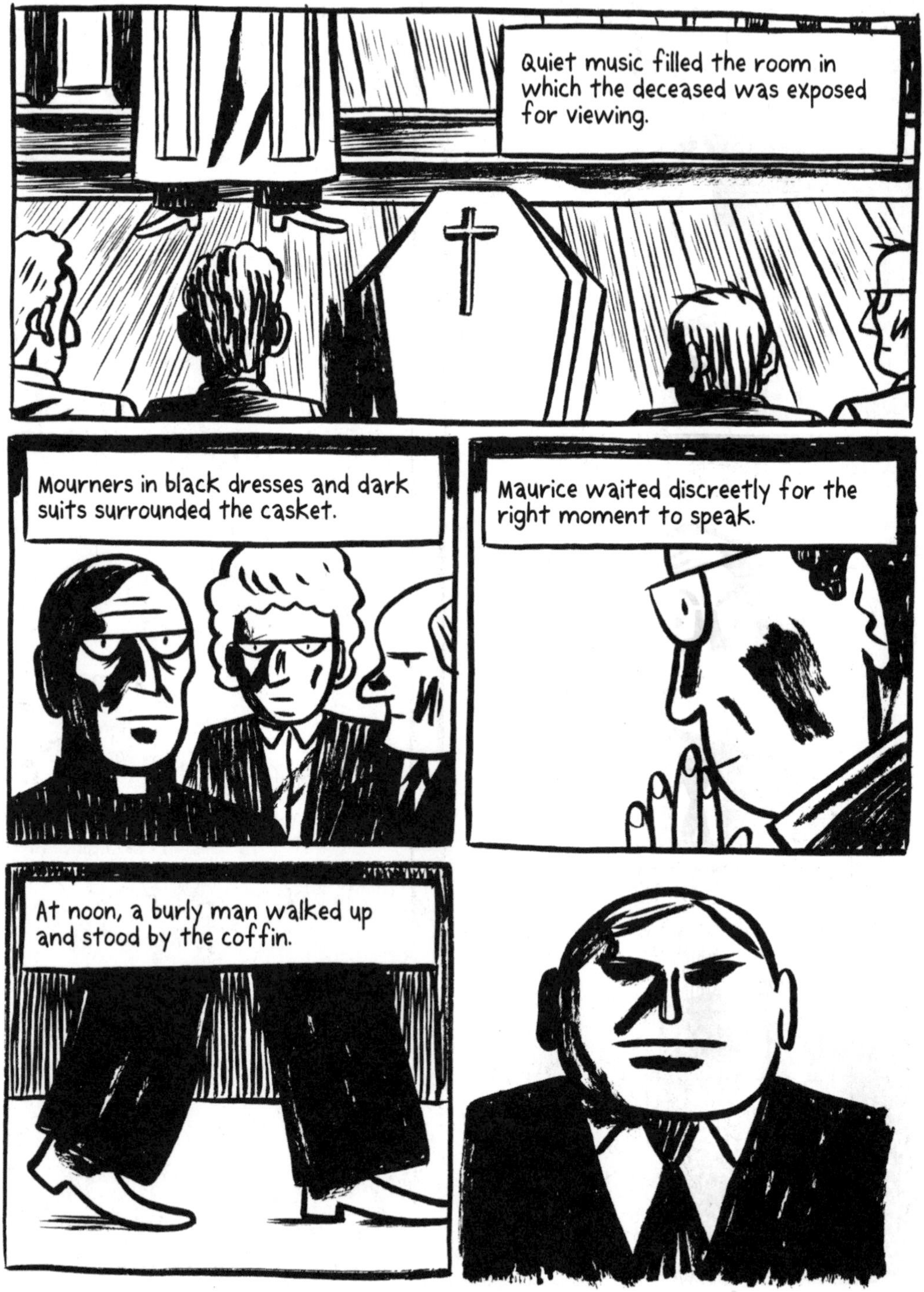
Quiet music filled the room in which the deceased was exposed for viewing.
Mourners in black dresses and dark suits surrounded the casket.
Maurice waited discreetly for the right moment to speak.
At noon, a burly man walked up and stood by the coffin.

If anyone would like to say something about Al, go ahead. Personally, I'd suggest you keep your trap shut!

Three behemoths with faces like pit bulls stood by my side. My father's men.

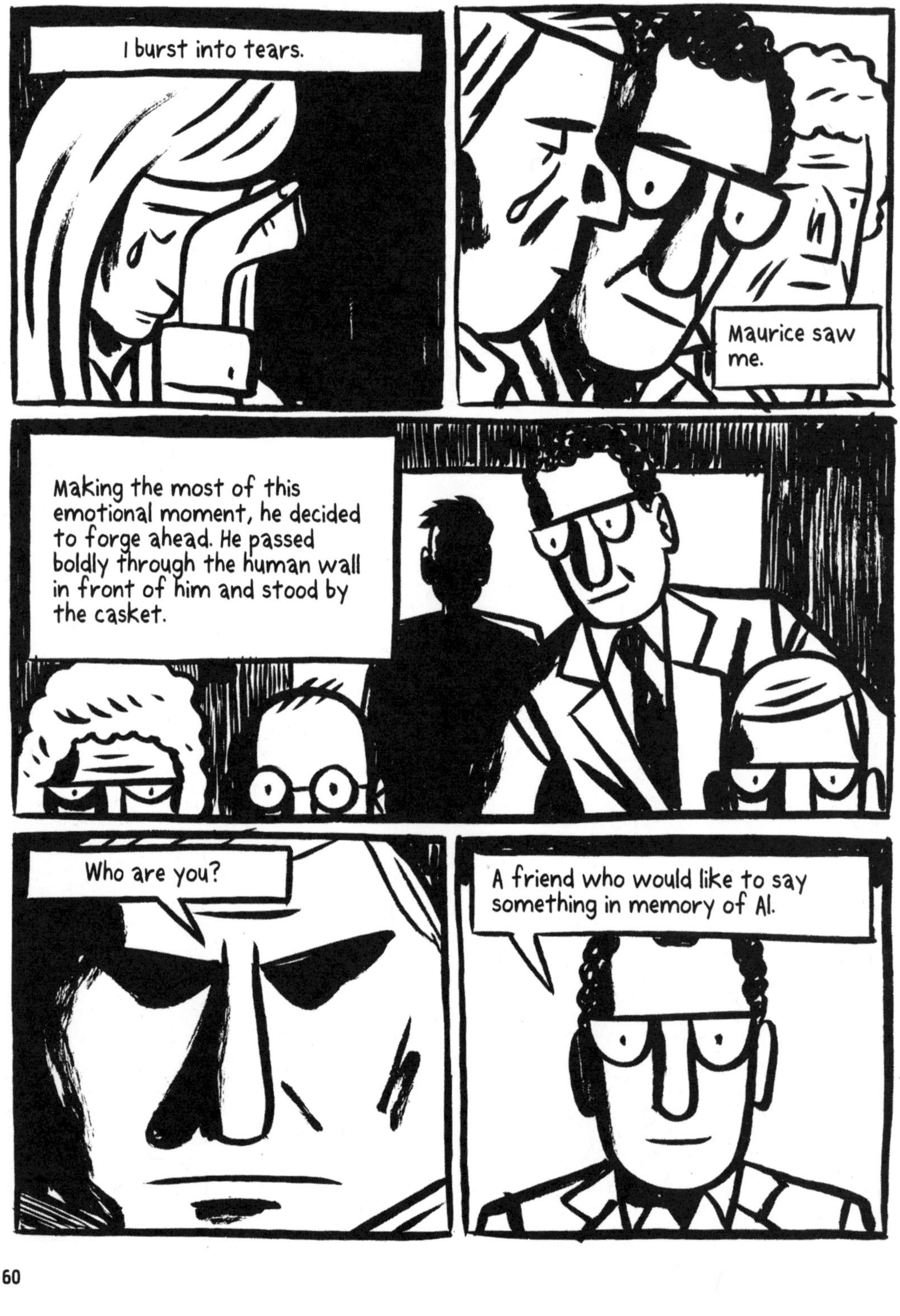
I burst into tears.
Maurice saw me.
Making the most of this emotional moment, he decided to forge ahead. He passed boldly through the human wall in front of him and stood by the casket.
Who are you?
A friend who would like to say something in memory of Al.

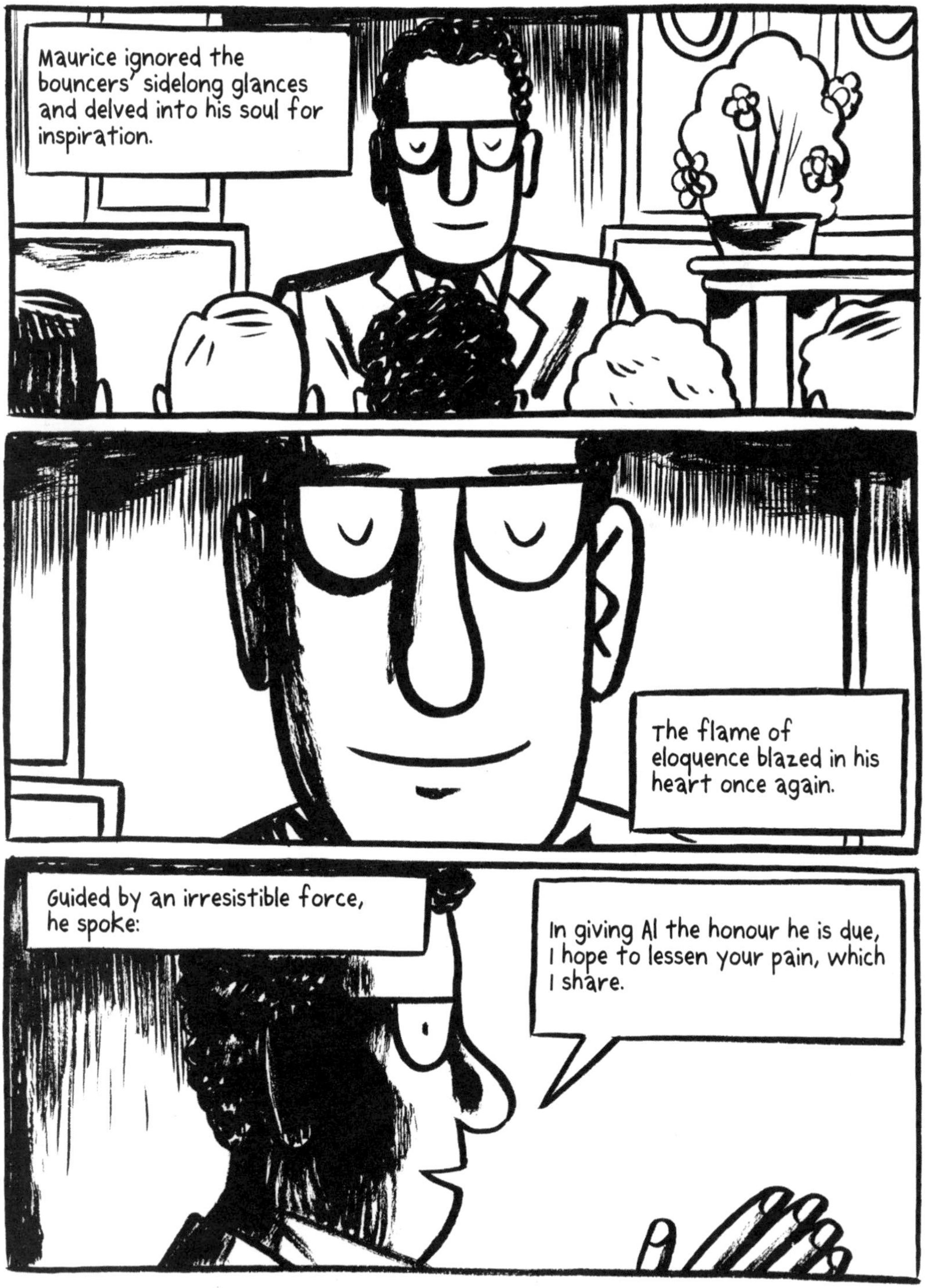
Maurice ignored the bouncers' sidelong glances and delved into his soul for inspiration.
The flame of eloquence blazed in his heart once again.
Guided by an irresistible force, he spoke:
In giving Al the honour he is due, I hope to lessen your pain, which I share.

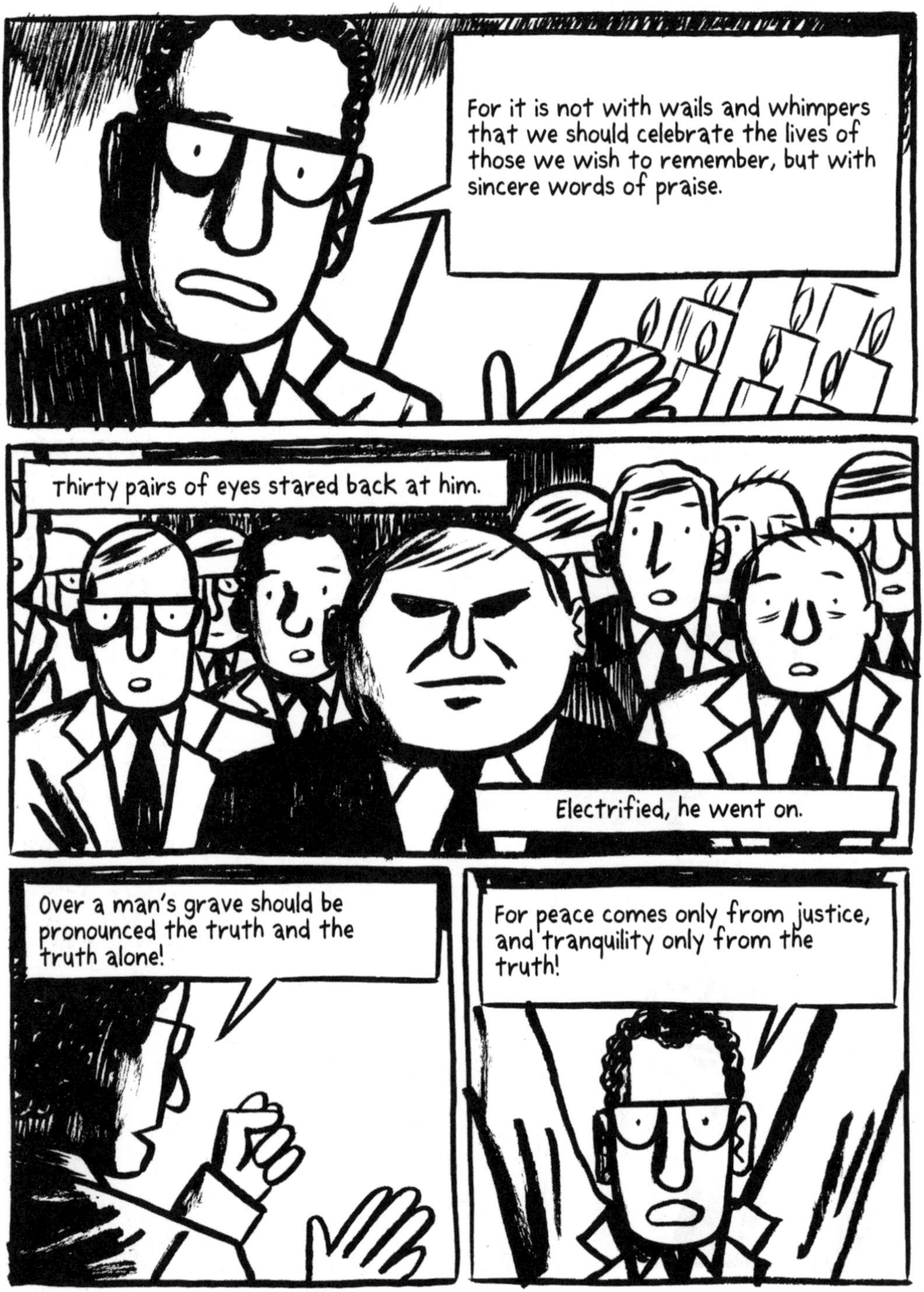
For it is not with wails and whimpers that we should celebrate the lives of those we wish to remember, but with sincere words of praise.
Thirty pairs of eyes stared back at him.
Electrified, he went on.
Over a man's grave should be pronounced the truth and the truth alone!
For peace comes only from justice, and tranquility only from the truth!

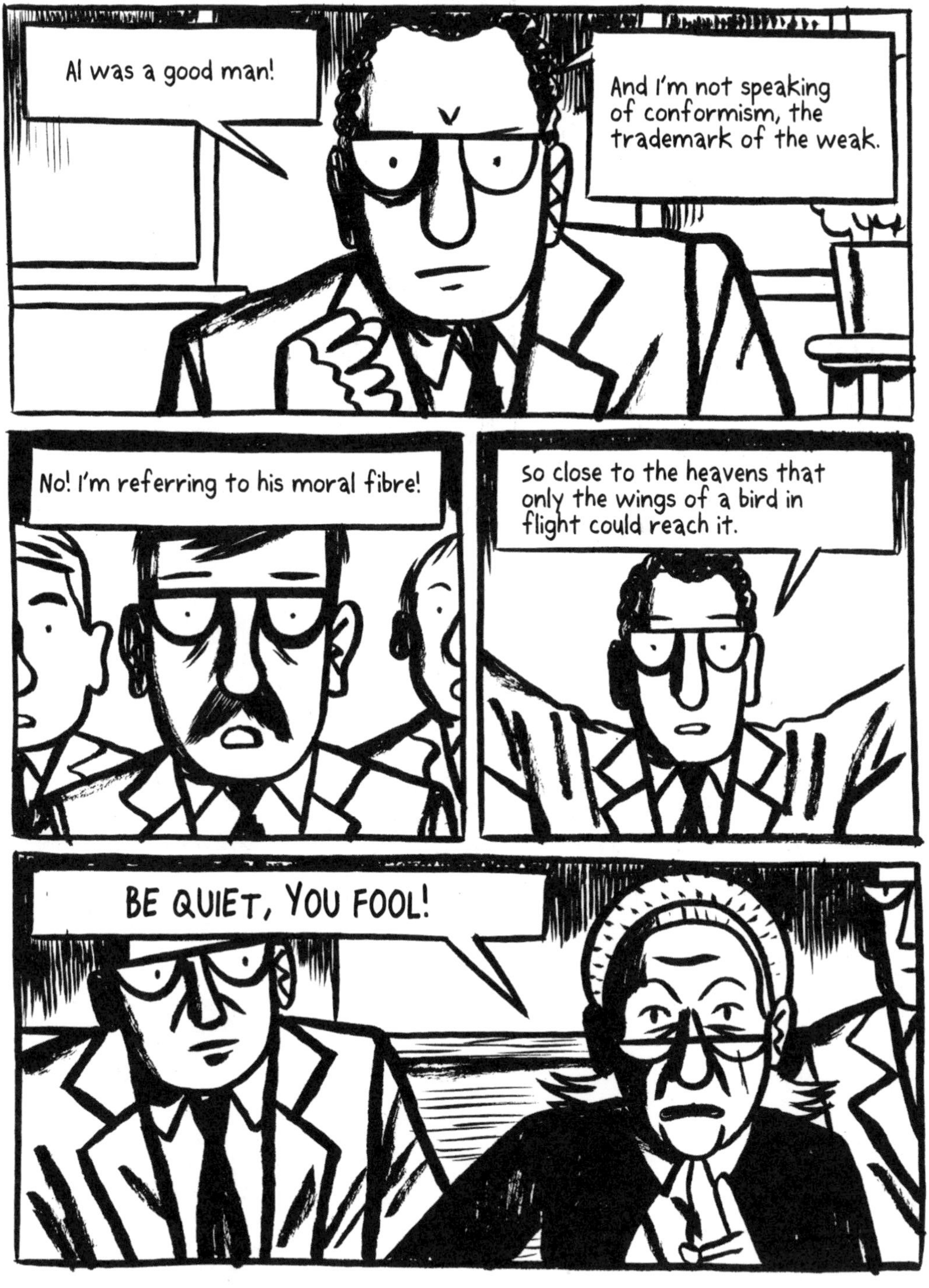

Al was a good man!
And I'm not speaking of conformism, the trademark of the weak.
No! I'm referring to his moral fibre!
So close to the heavens that only the wings of a bird in flight could reach it.
BE QUIET, YOU FOOL!

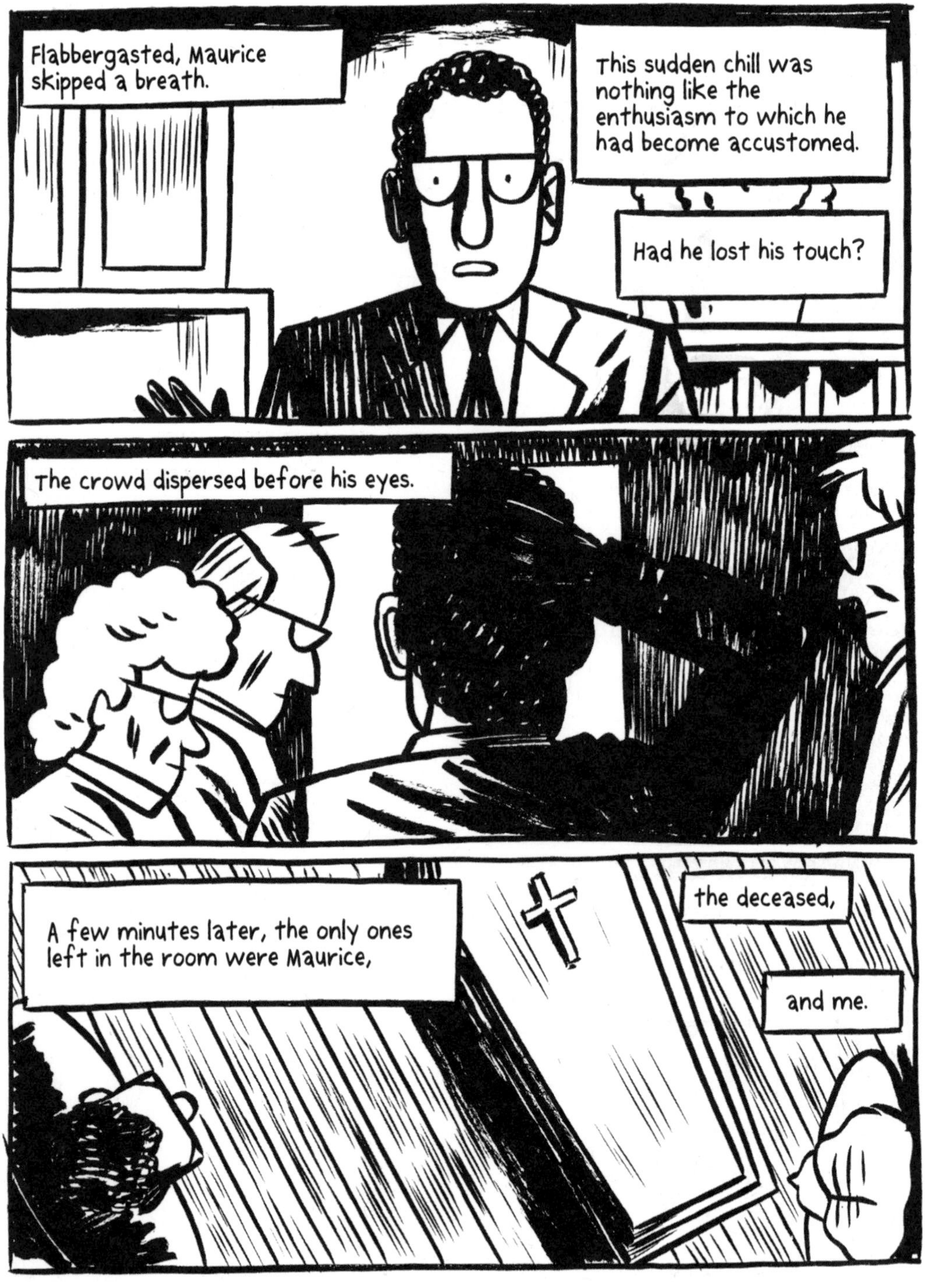
Flabbergasted, Maurice skipped a breath.
This sudden chill was nothing like the enthusiasm to which he had become accustomed.
Had he lost his touch?
The crowd dispersed before his eyes.
A few minutes later, the only ones left in the room were Maurice,
the deceased,
and me.

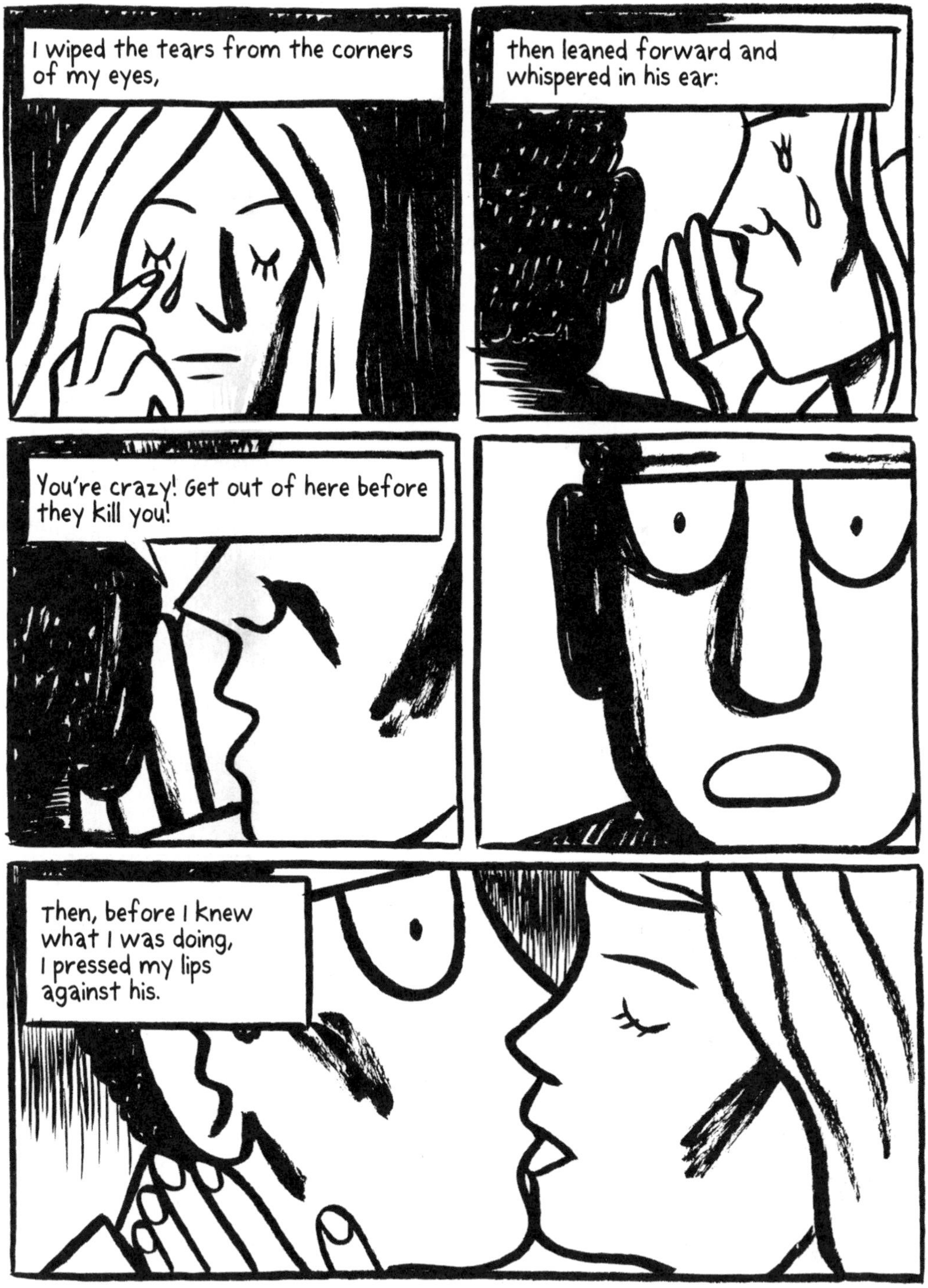
I wiped the tears from the corners of my eyes,
then leaned forward and whispered in his ear:
You're crazy! Get out of here before they kill you!
Then, before I knew what I was doing, I pressed my lips against his.

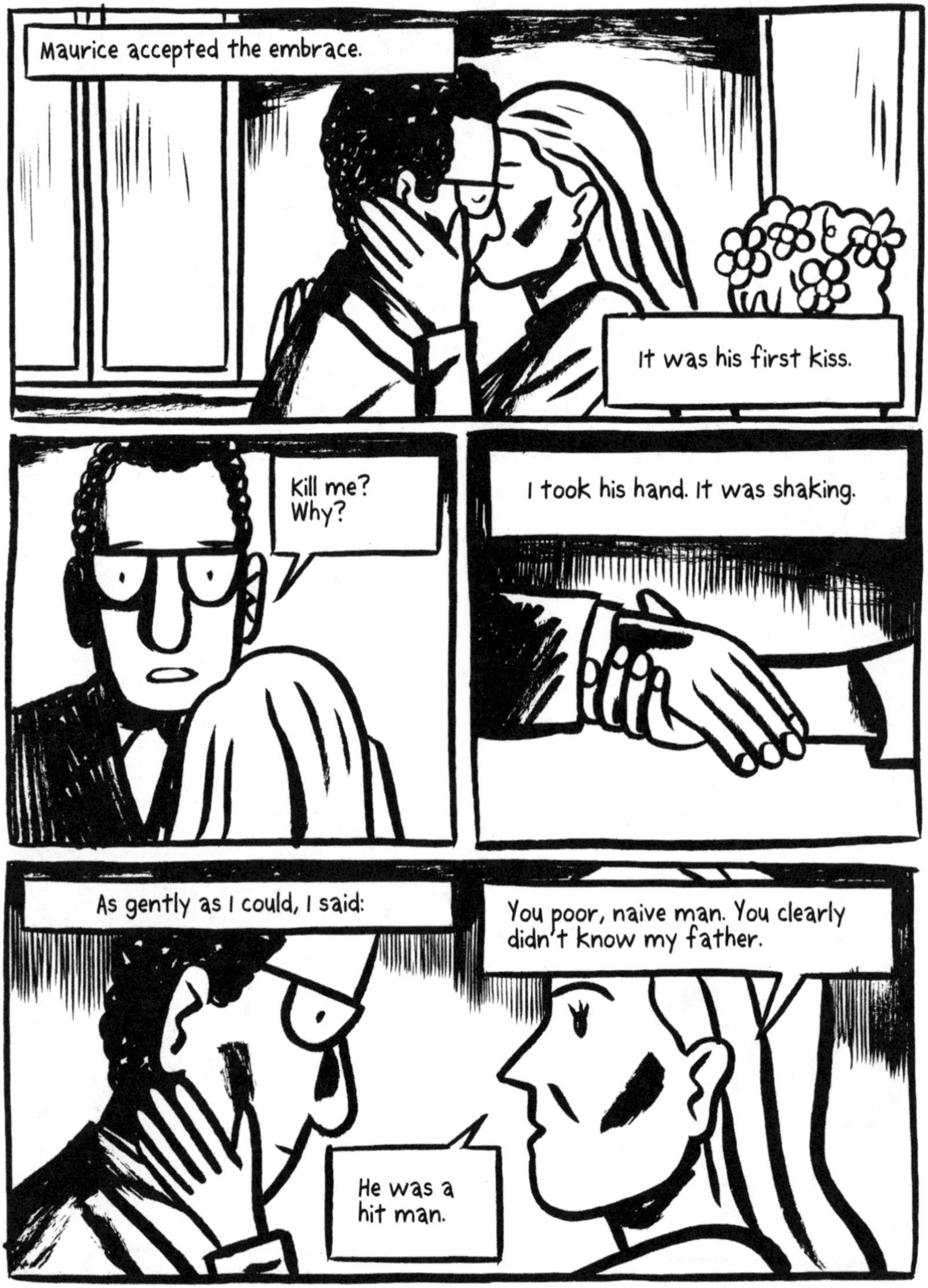

Maurice accepted the embrace.
It was his first kiss.
Kill me? Why?
I took his hand. It was shaking.
As gently as I could, I said:
You poor, naive man. You clearly didn't know my father.
He was a hit man.

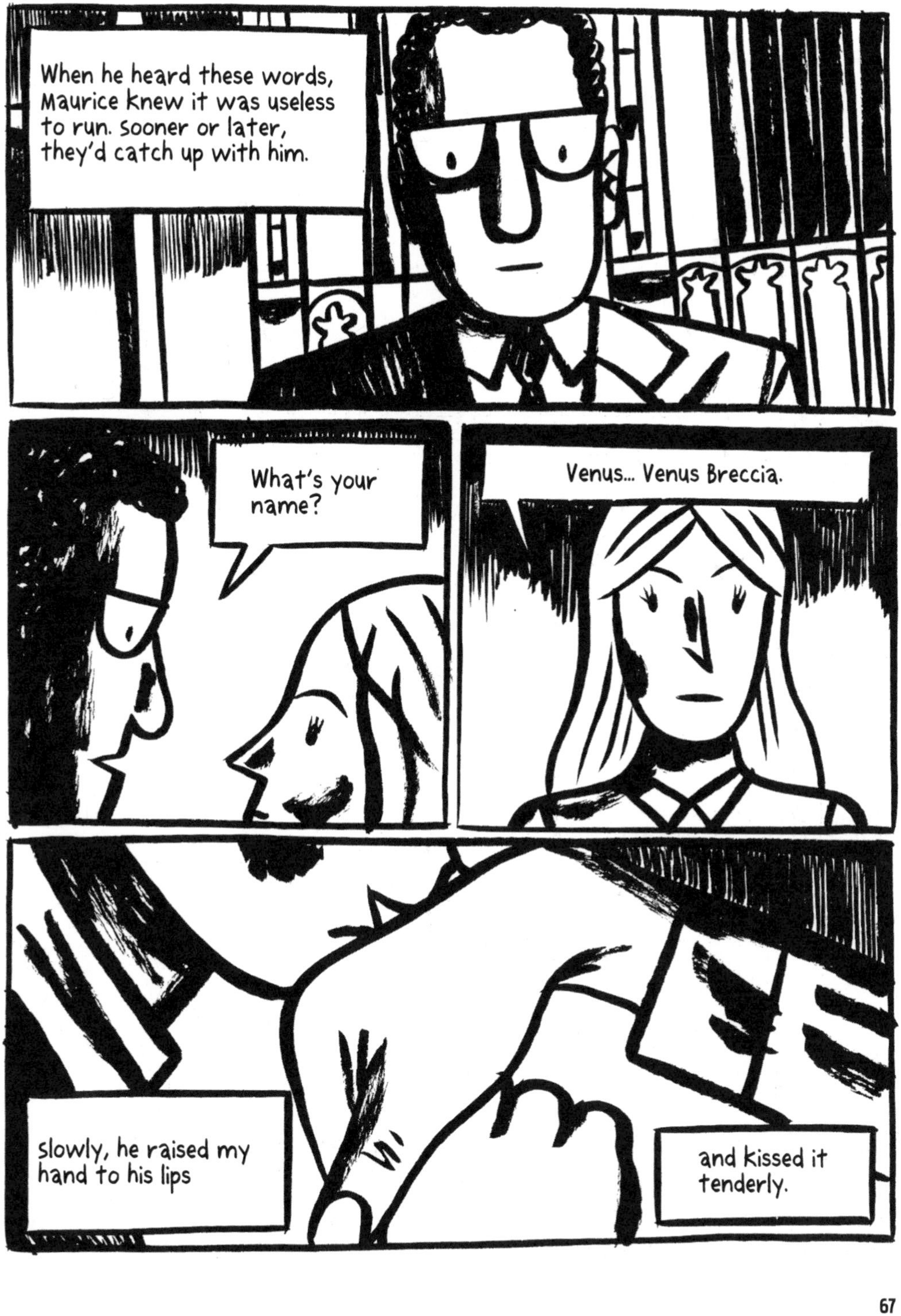
When he heard these words, Maurice knew it was useless to run. Sooner or later, they'd catch up with him.
What's your name?
Venus... Venus Breccia.
Slowly, he raised my hand to his lips
and kissed it tenderly.

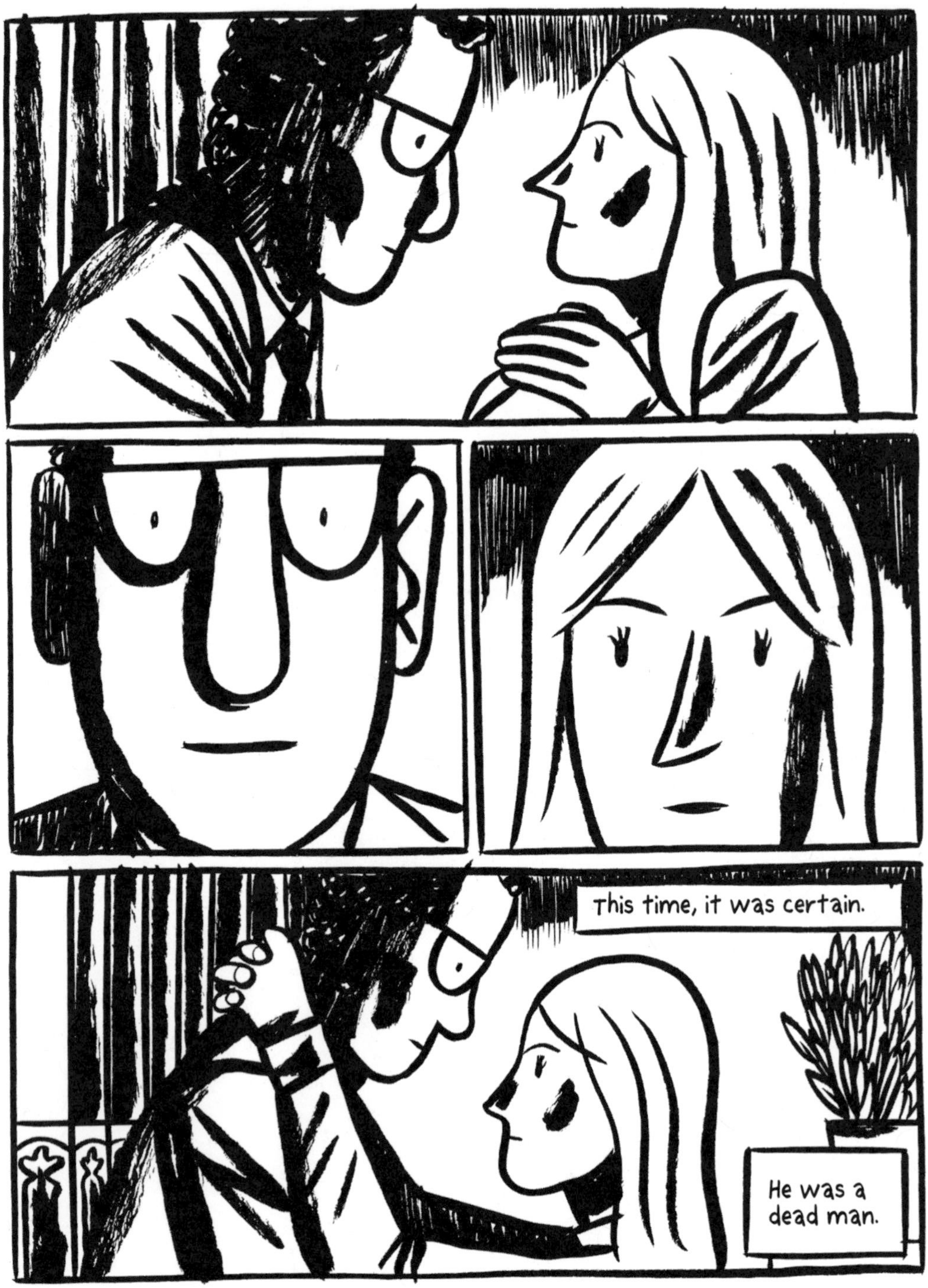
This time, it was certain.
He was a dead man.

# Chapter 4

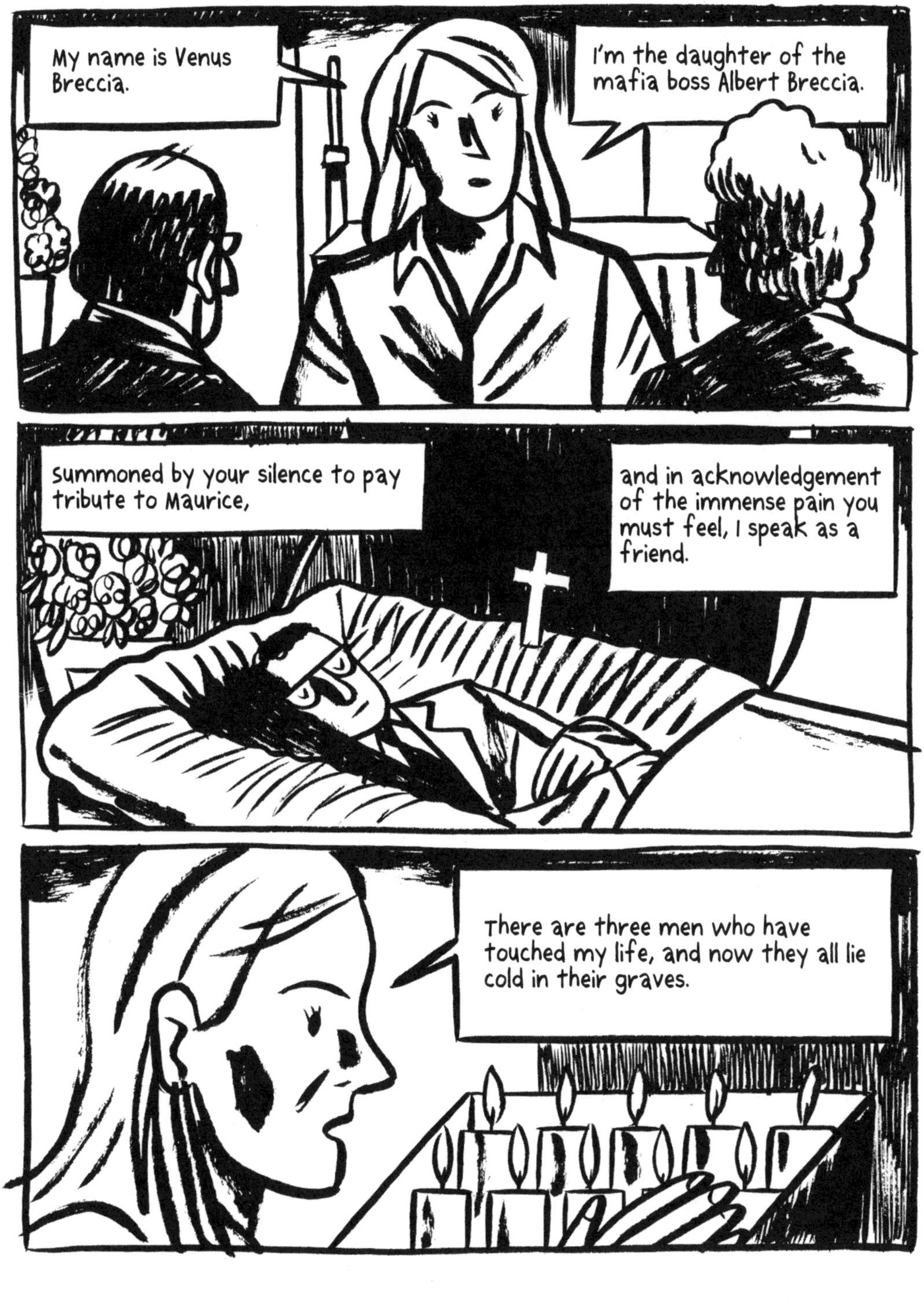
My name is Venus Breccia.
I'm the daughter of the mafia boss Albert Breccia.
summoned by your silence to pay tribute to Maurice,
and in acknowledgement of the immense pain you must feel, I speak as a friend.
There are three men who have touched my life, and now they all lie cold in their graves.

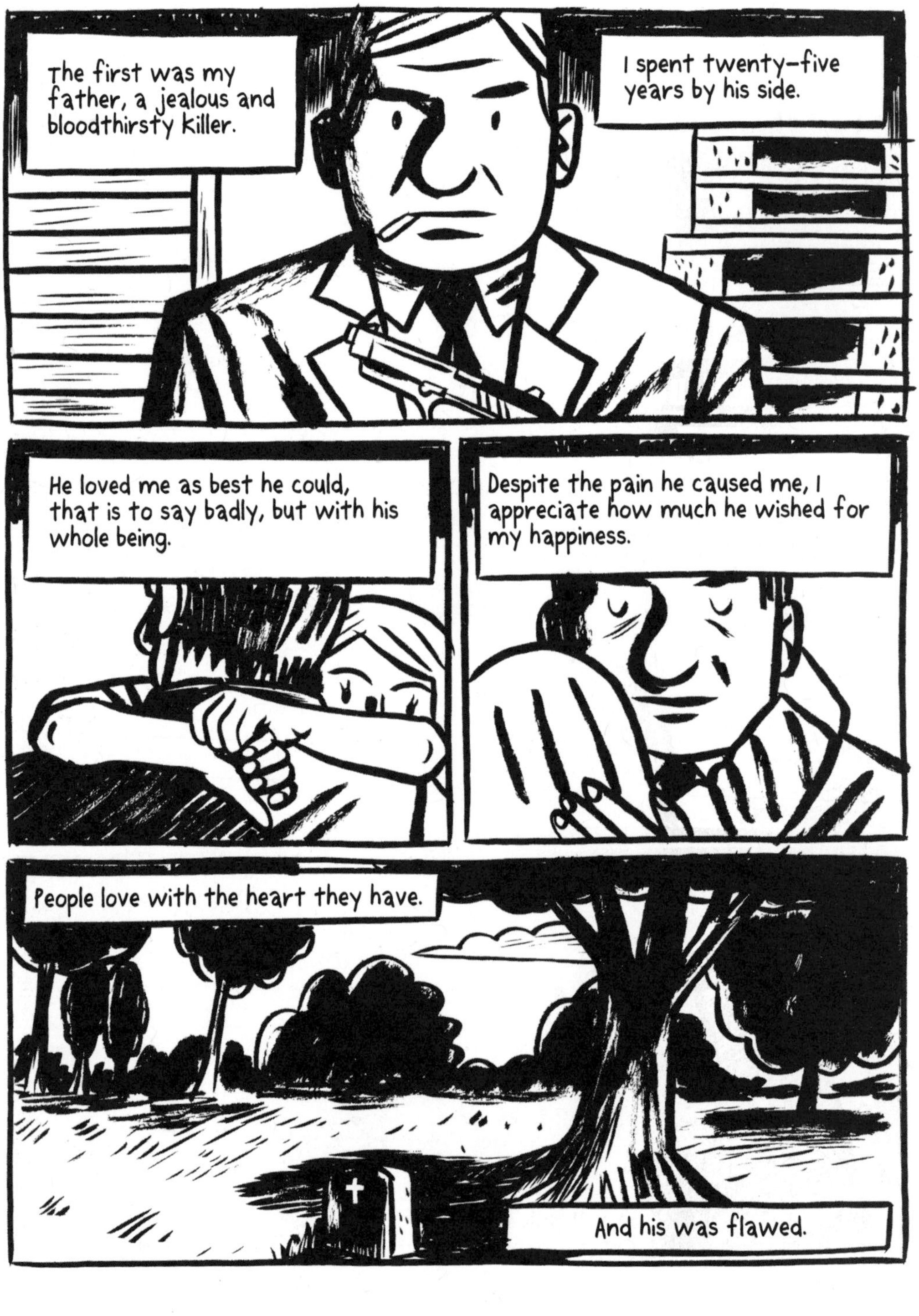
The first was my father, a jealous and bloodthirsty killer.
I spent twenty-five years by his side.
He loved me as best he could, that is to say badly, but with his whole being.
Despite the pain he caused me, I appreciate how much he wished for my happiness.
People love with the heart they have.
And his was flawed.

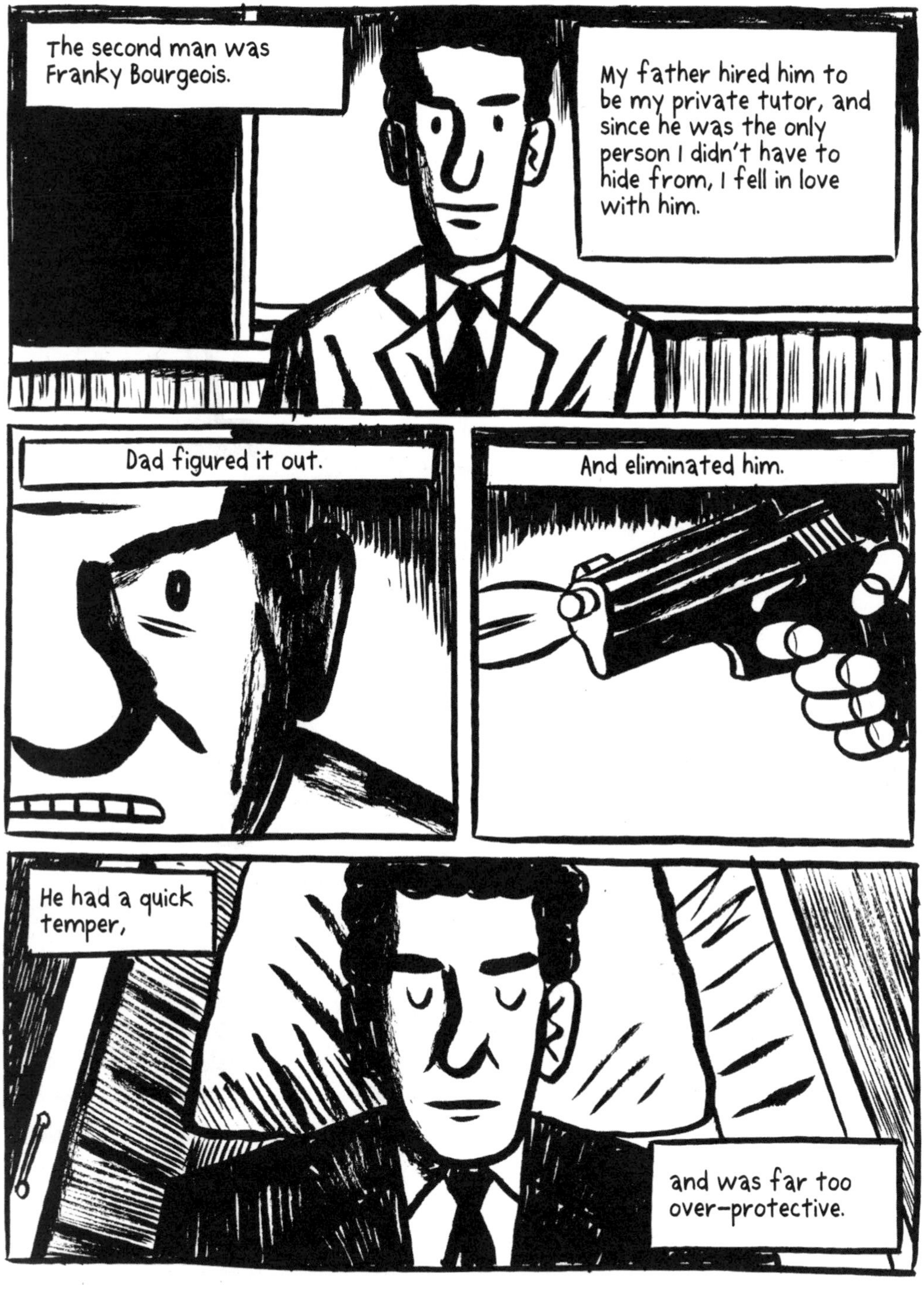
The second man was Franky Bourgeois.
My father hired him to be my private tutor, and since he was the only person I didn't have to hide from, I fell in love with him.
Dad figured it out.
And eliminated him.
He had a quick temper,
and was far too over-protective.

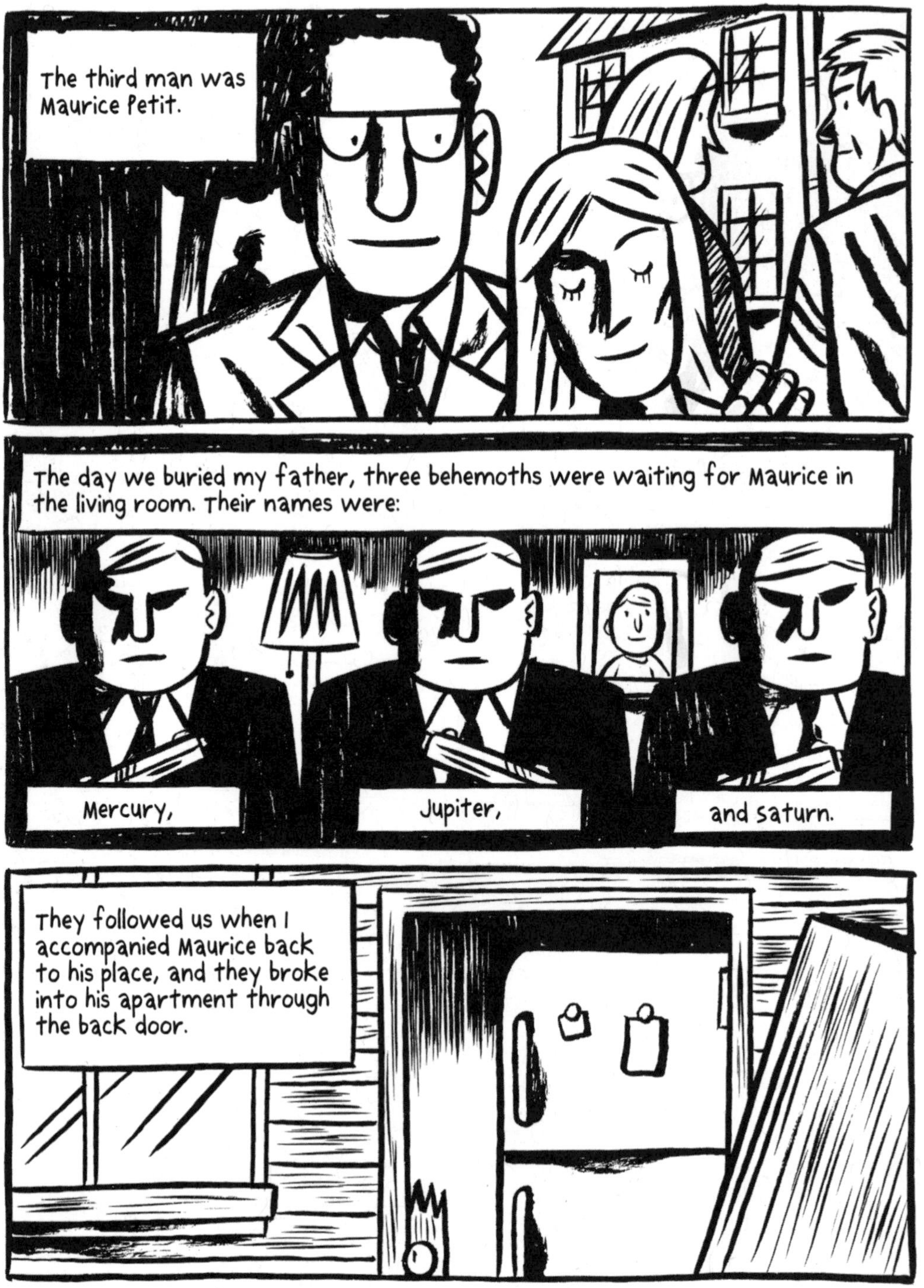
The third man was Maurice Petit.
The day we buried my father, three behemoths were waiting for Maurice in the living room. Their names were:
Mercury,
Jupiter,
and saturn.
They followed us when I accompanied Maurice back to his place, and they broke into his apartment through the back door.

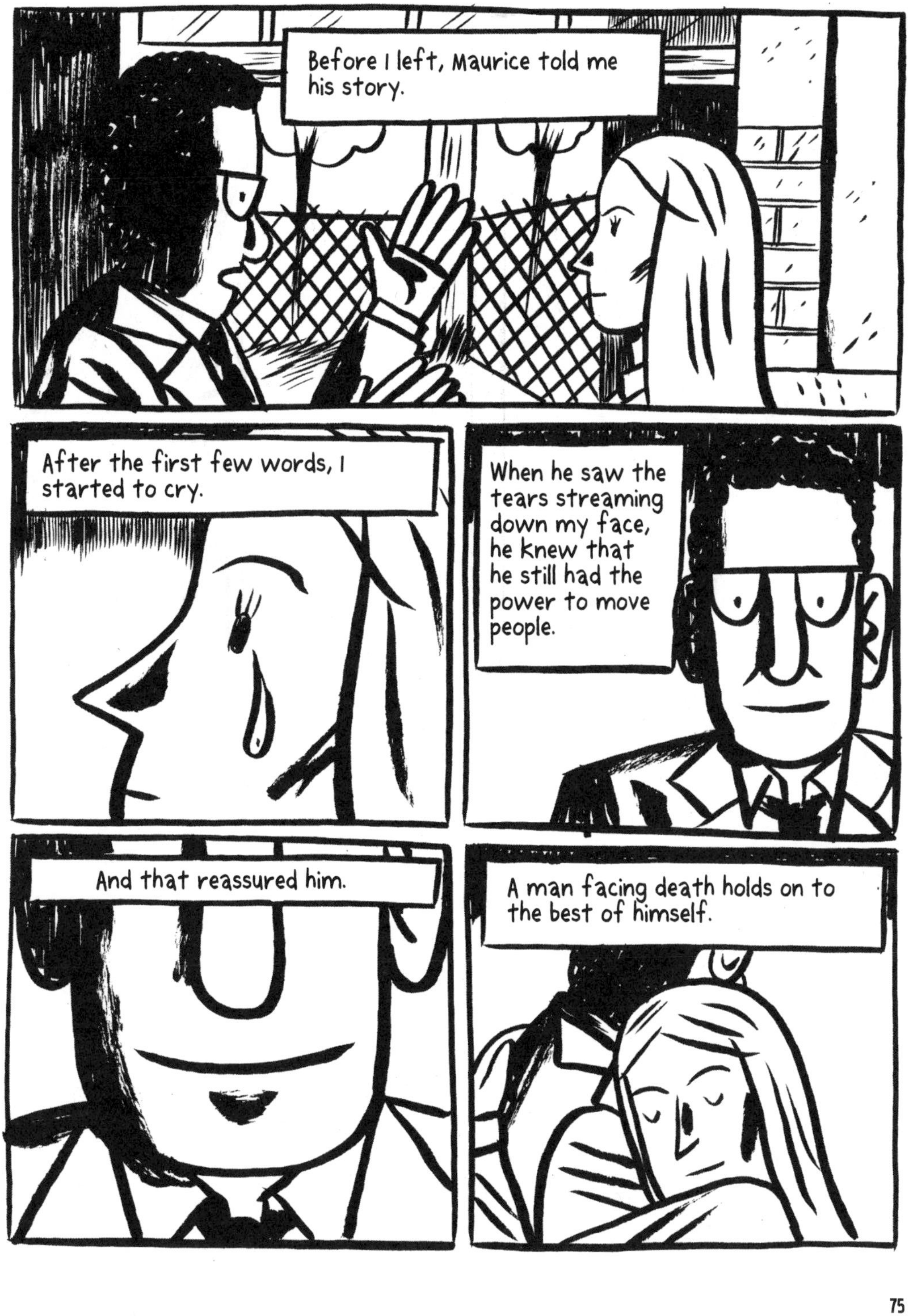
Before I left, Maurice told me his story.
After the first few words, I started to cry.
When he saw the tears streaming down my face, he knew that he still had the power to move people.
And that reassured him.
A man facing death holds on to the best of himself.

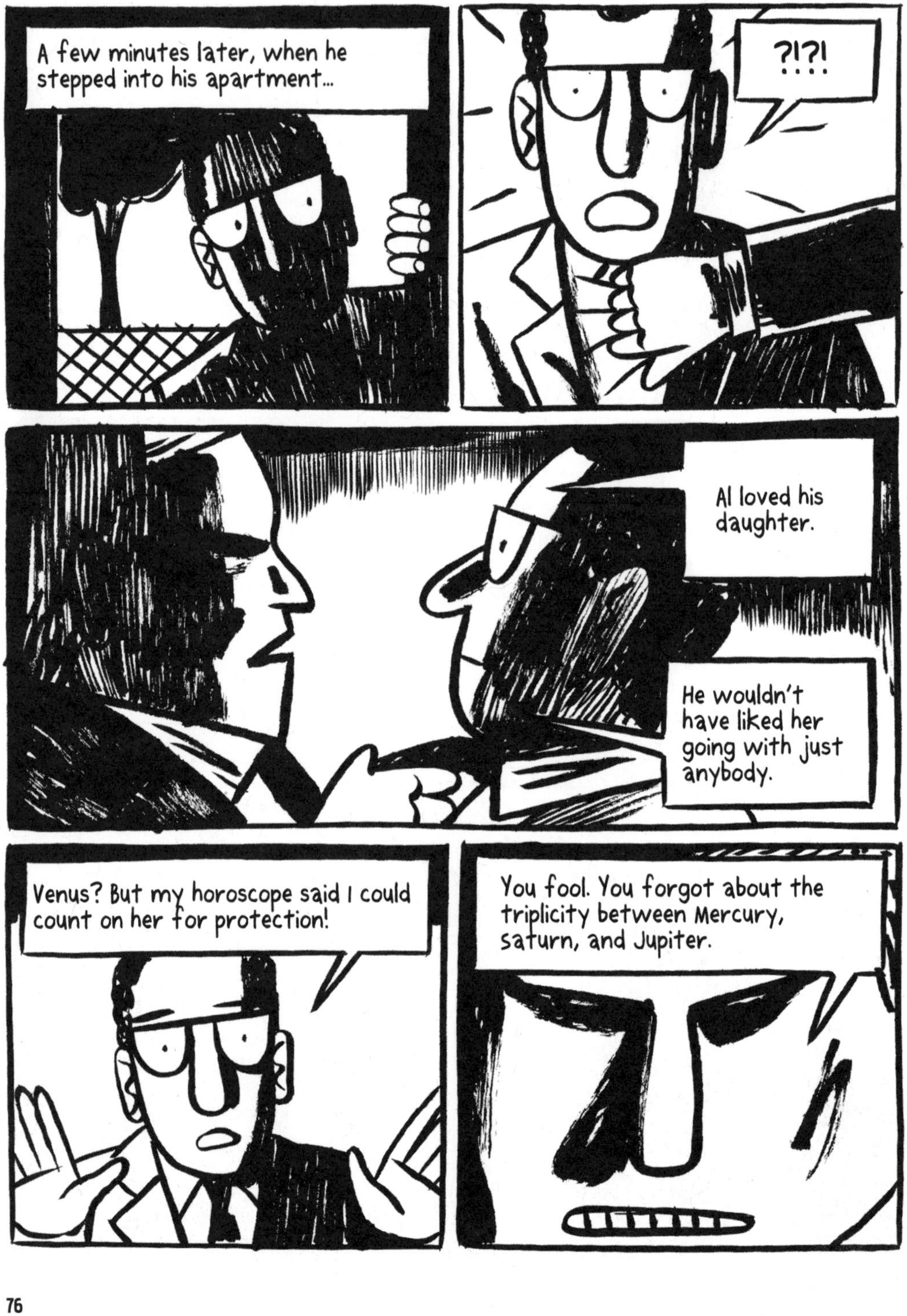

A few minutes later, when he stepped into his apartment...
?!?!
Al loved his daughter.
He wouldn't have liked her going with just anybody.
Venus? But my horoscope said I could count on her for protection!
You fool. You forgot about the triplicity between Mercury, Saturn, and Jupiter.

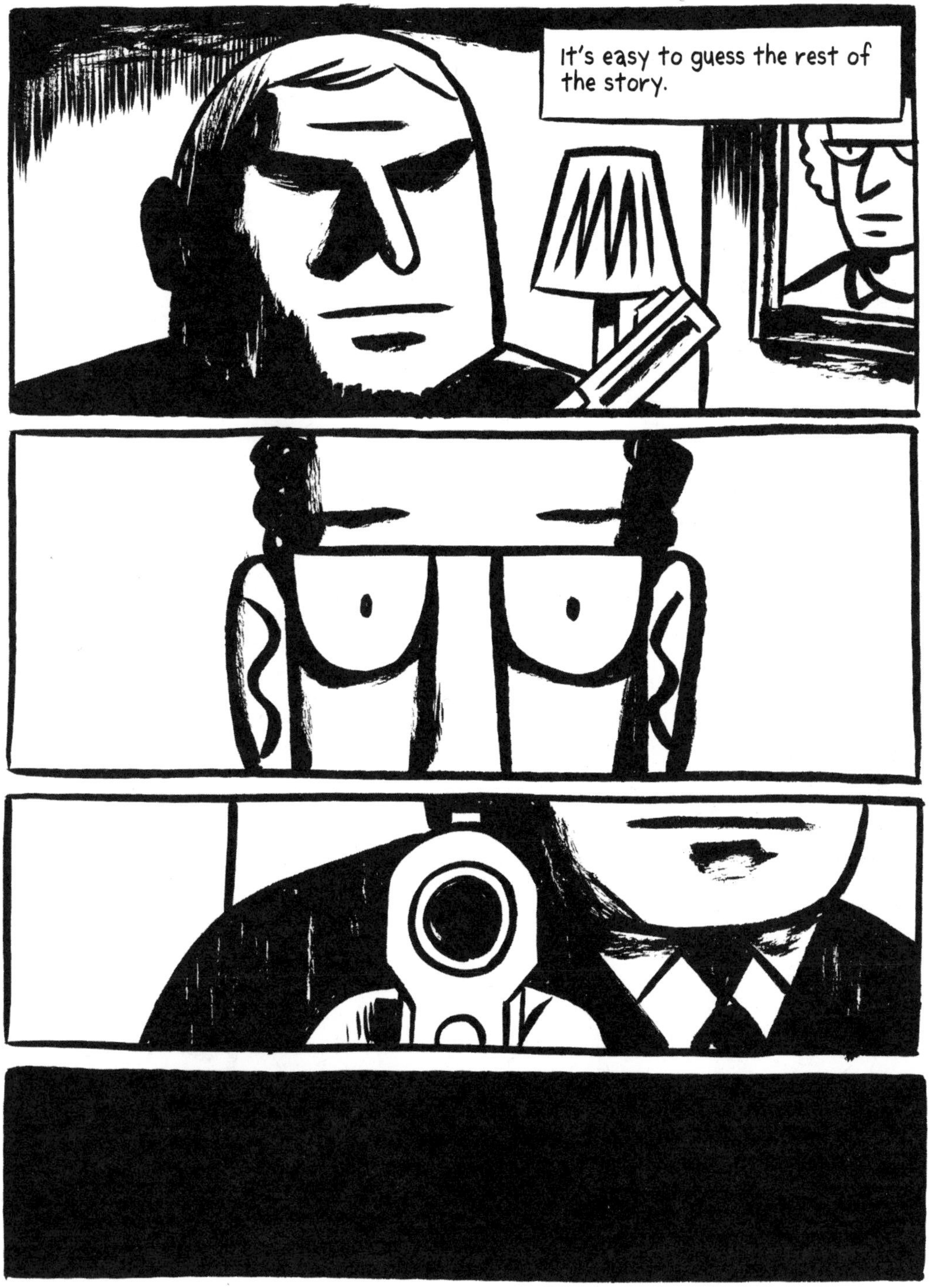
It's easy to guess the rest of the story.

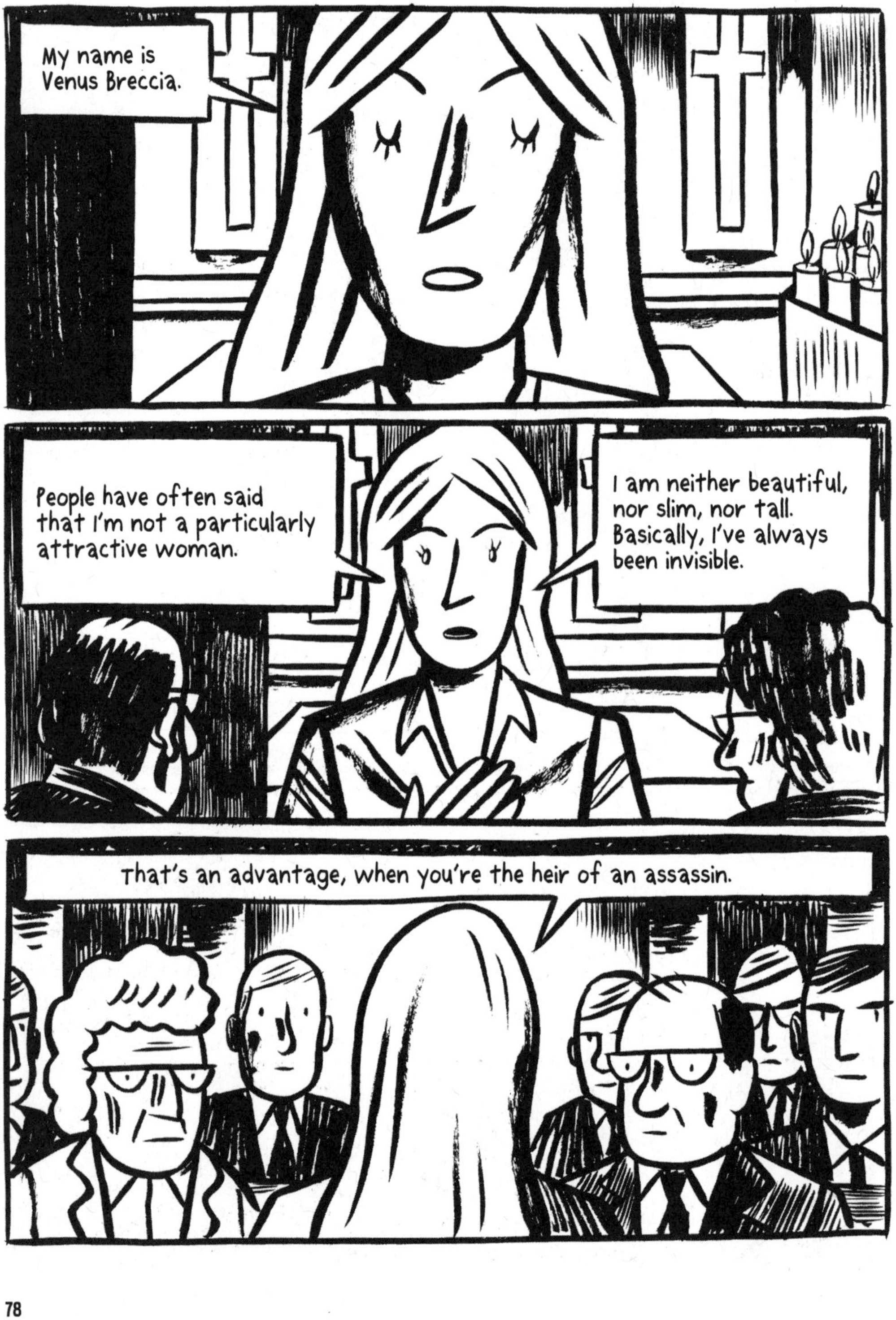

My name is Venus Breccia.
People have often said that I'm not a particularly attractive woman.
I am neither beautiful, nor slim, nor tall. Basically, I've always been invisible.
That's an advantage, when you're the heir of an assassin.

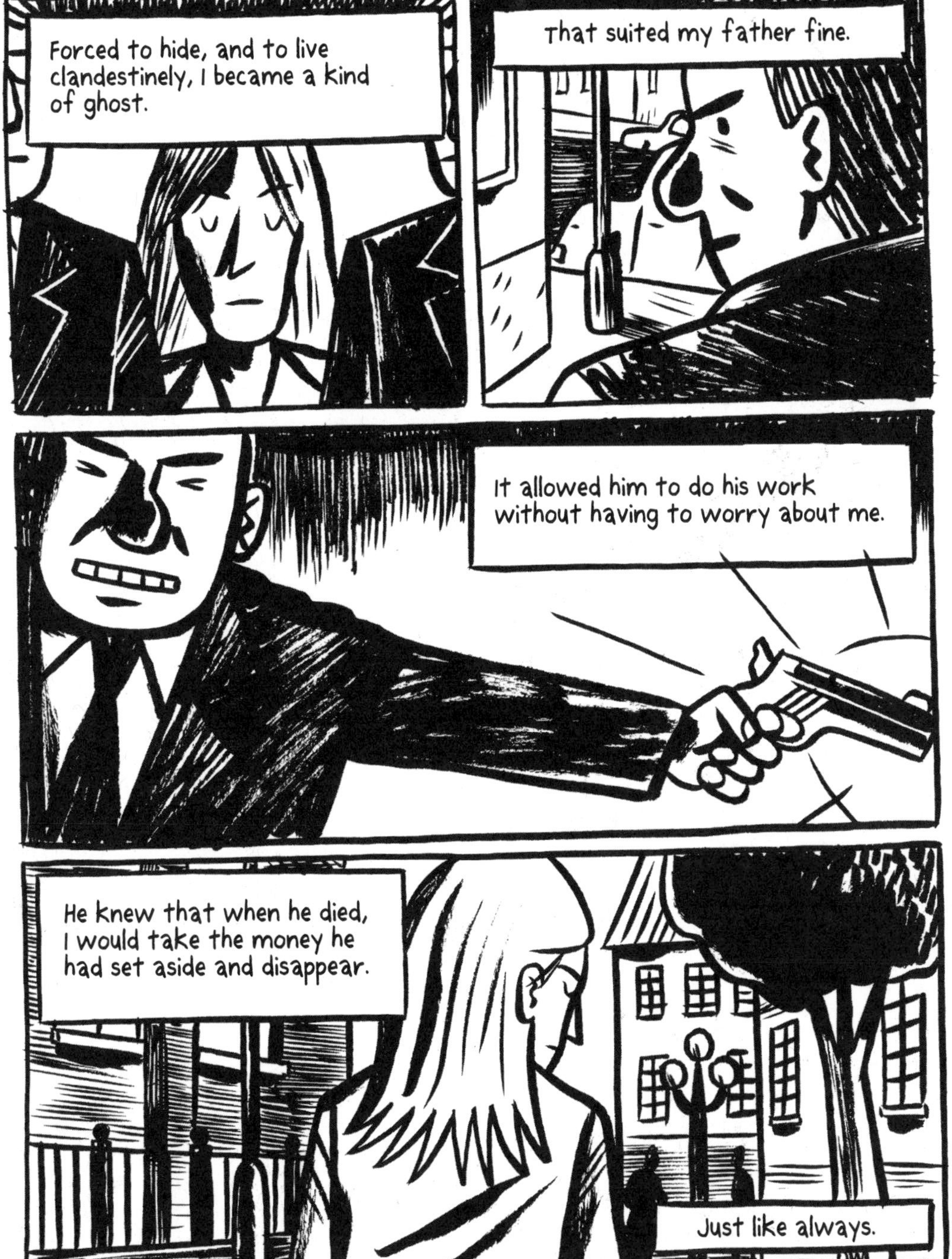

Forced to hide, and to live clandestinely, I became a kind of ghost.
That suited my father fine.
It allowed him to do his work without having to worry about me.
He knew that when he died, I would take the money he had set aside and disappear.
Just like always.

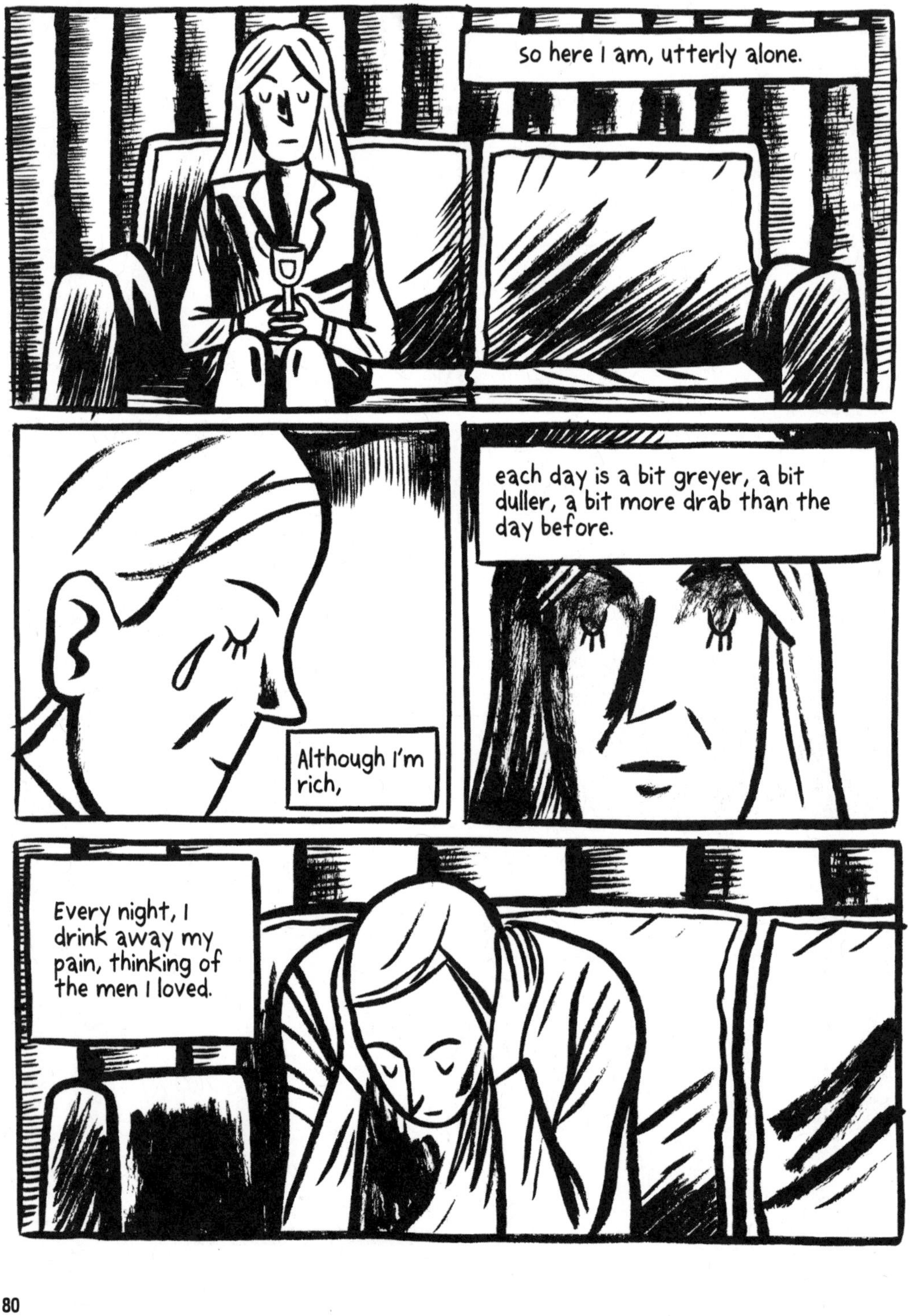
so here I am, utterly alone.
Although I'm rich,
each day is a bit greyer, a bit duller, a bit more drab than the day before.
Every night, I drink away my pain, thinking of the men I loved.

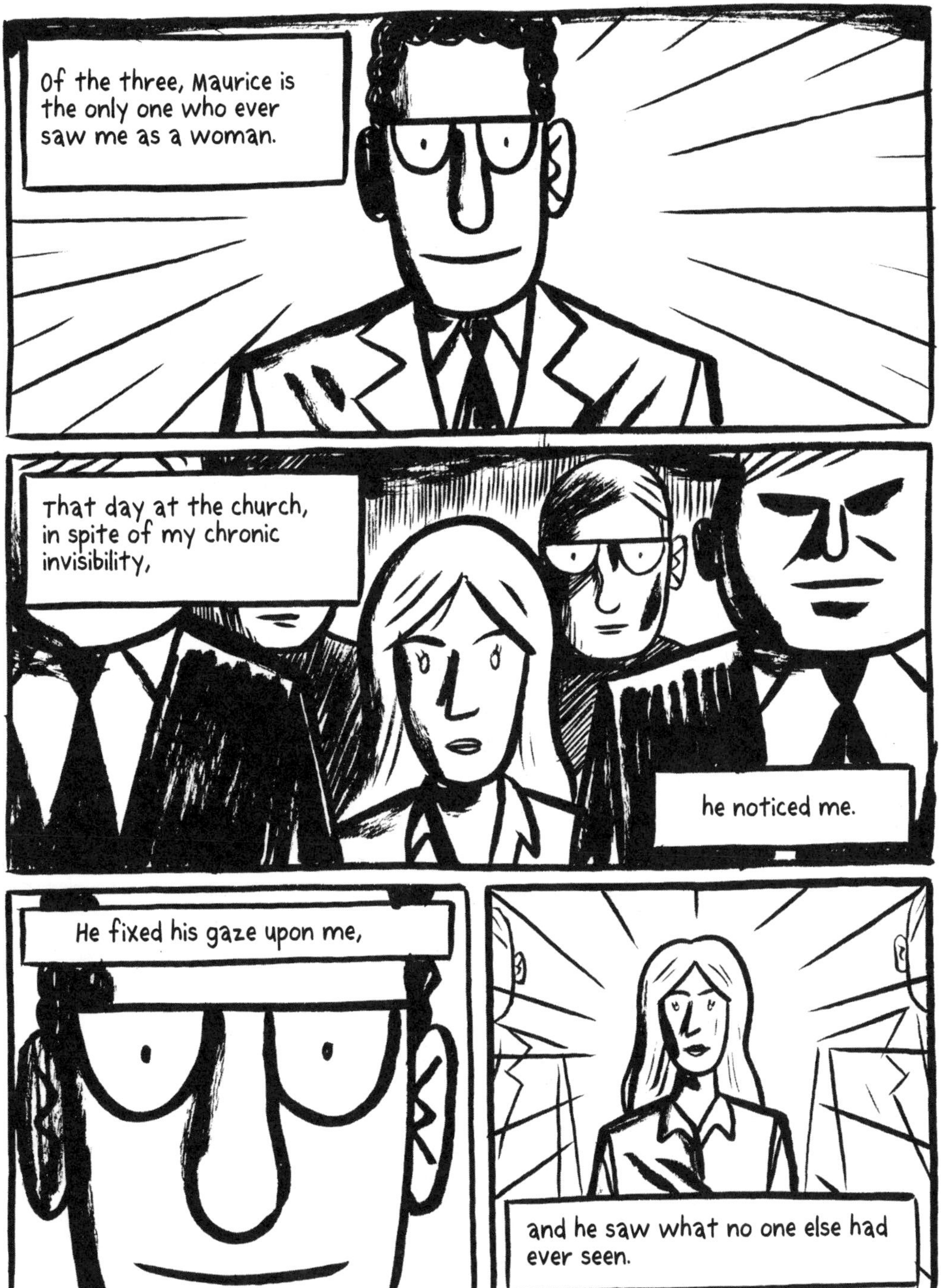
Of the three, Maurice is the only one who ever saw me as a woman.
That day at the church, in spite of my chronic invisibility,
he noticed me.
He fixed his gaze upon me,
and he saw what no one else had ever seen.

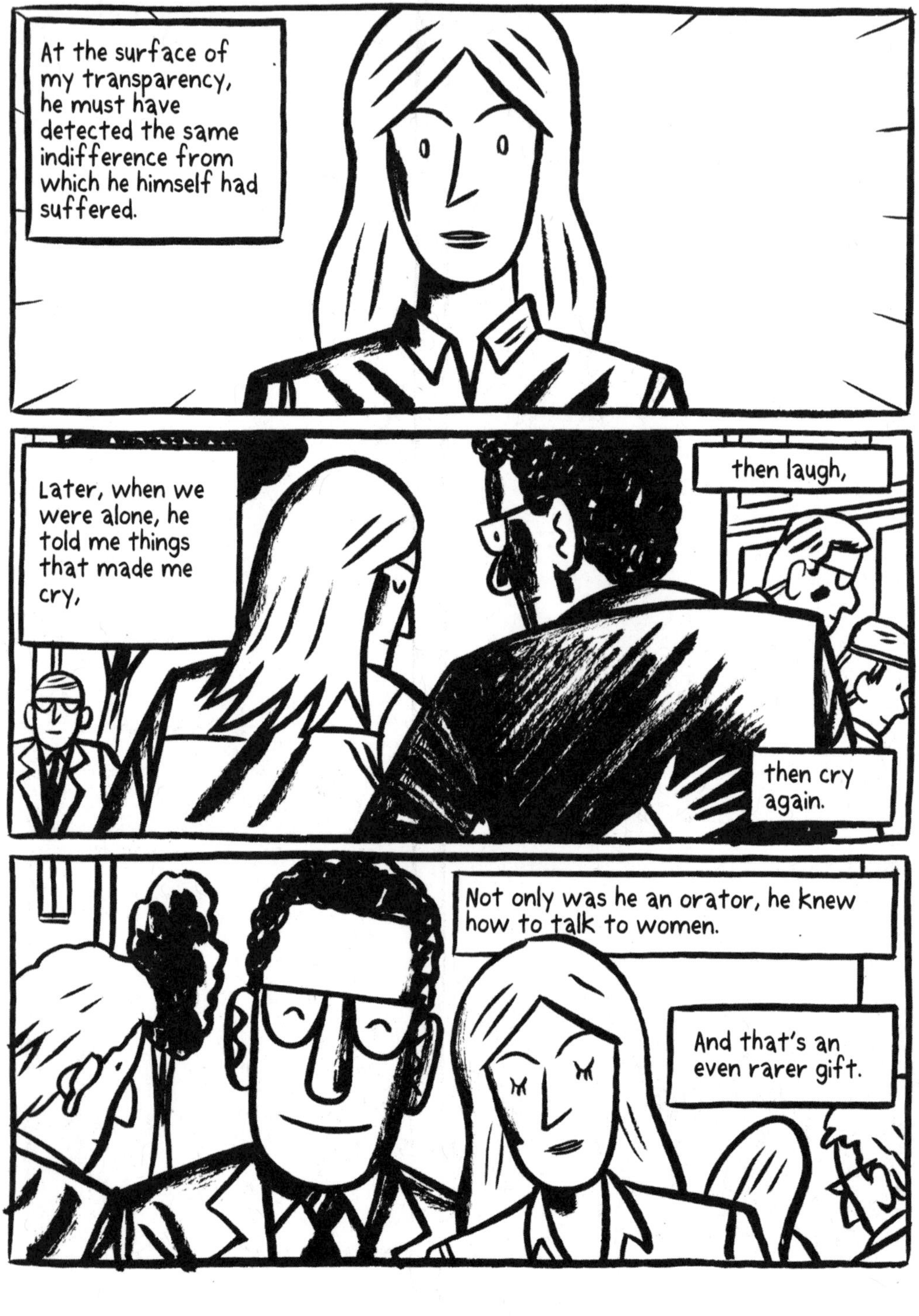
At the surface of my transparency, he must have detected the same indifference from which he himself had suffered.
Later, when we were alone, he told me things that made me cry,
then laugh,
then cry again.
Not only was he an orator, he knew how to talk to women.
And that's an even rarer gift.

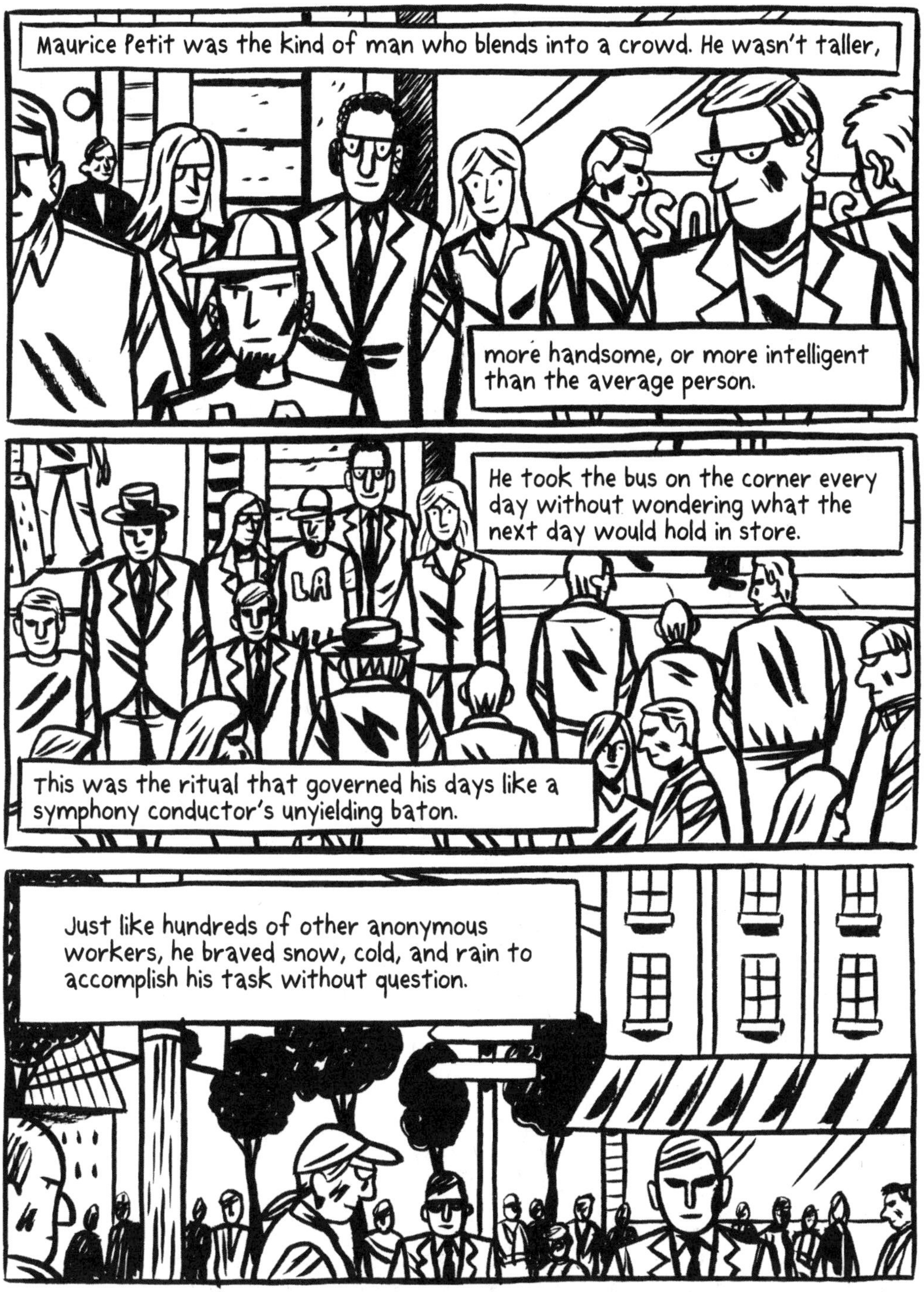

Maurice Petit was the kind of man who blends into a crowd. He wasn't taller,
more handsome, or more intelligent than the average person.
He took the bus on the corner every day without wondering what the next day would hold in store.
LA
This was the ritual that governed his days like a symphony conductor's unyielding baton.
Just like hundreds of other anonymous workers, he braved snow, cold, and rain to accomplish his task without question.

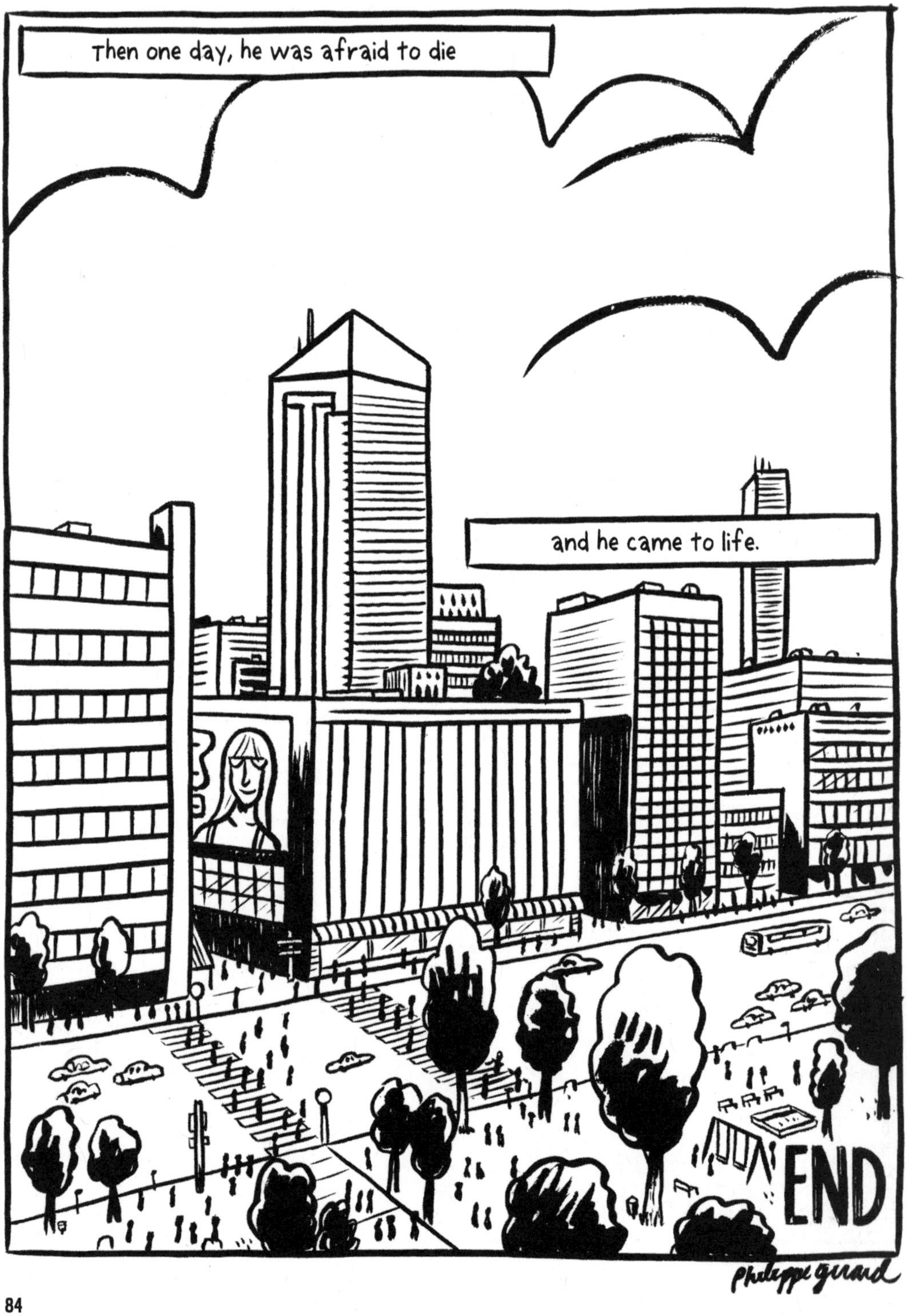
Then one day, he was afraid to die
and he came to life.
END

Philippe Girard